READINGS ON

ARTHUR MILLER

OTHER TITLES IN THE GREENHAVEN PRESS
LITERARY COMPANION SERIES:

AMERICAN AUTHORS

Nathaniel Hawthorne
Ernest Hemingway
Herman Melville
John Steinbeck
Mark Twain

BRITISH AUTHORS

Jane Austen

WORLD AUTHORS

Sophocles

BRITISH LITERATURE

The Canterbury Tales
Shakespeare: The Comedies
Shakespeare: The Sonnets
Shakespeare: The Tragedies

THE GREENHAVEN PRESS
Literary Companion
TO AMERICAN AUTHORS

ARTHUR MILLER

David Bender, *Publisher*
Bruno Leone, *Executive Editor*
Scott Barbour, *Managing Editor*
Bonnie Szumski, *Series Editor*
Thomas Siebold, *Book Editor*

Greenhaven Press, San Diego, CA

Library of Congress Cataloging-in-Publication Data

Readings on Arthur Miller / Thomas Siebold, book editor.
     p.   cm. — (The Greenhaven Press literary
companion to American authors)
   Includes bibliographical references and index.
   ISBN 1-56510-580-X (lib. bdg. : alk. paper). —
ISBN 1-56510-579-6 (pbk. : alk. paper)
   1. Miller, Arthur, 1915–   —Criticism and interpretation. I. Siebold, Thomas. II. Series.
PS3525.I5156Z865   1997
812'.52–dc20   96-36477
                                                CIP

Cover photo: UPI/Bettmann

Copyright ©1997 by Greenhaven Press, Inc.
PO Box 289009
San Diego, CA 92198-9009
Printed in the U.S.A.

> **"Criticism hurt me when I had failures. I thought: I'll never write another play. But I'm an alligator. Only the alligators remain. The others get out of the water."**

Arthur Miller, **The Observer,**
April 5, 1987

Contents

Chapter 1: A General Introduction to the Playwright

Chapter 2: Major Themes in Miller's Plays

Chapter 4: *The Crucible*

Chapter 5: Other Works

FOREWORD

*"'Tis the good reader that
makes the good book."*

Ralph Waldo Emerson

The story's bare facts are simple: The captain, an old and scarred seafarer, walks with a peg leg made of whale ivory. He relentlessly drives his crew to hunt the world's oceans for the great white whale that crippled him. After a long search, the ship encounters the whale and a fierce battle ensues. Finally the captain drives his harpoon into the whale, but the harpoon line catches the captain about the neck and drags him to his death.

A simple story, a straightforward plot—yet, since the 1851 publication of Herman Melville's *Moby-Dick*, readers and critics have found many meanings in the struggle between Captain Ahab and the whale. To some, the novel is a cautionary tale that depicts how Ahab's obsession with revenge leads to his insanity and death. Others believe that the whale represents the unknowable secrets of the universe and that Ahab is a tragic hero who dares to challenge fate by attempting to discover this knowledge. Perhaps Melville intended Ahab as a criticism of Americans' tendency to become involved in well-intentioned but irrational causes. Or did Melville model Ahab after himself, letting his fictional character express his anger at what he perceived as a cruel and distant god?

Although literary critics disagree over the meaning of *Moby-Dick*, readers do not need to choose one particular interpretation in order to gain an understanding of Melville's novel. Instead, by examining various analyses, they can gain

10

numerous insights into the issues that lie under the surface of the basic plot. Studying the writings of literary critics can also aid readers in making their own assessments of *Moby-Dick* and other literary works and in developing analytical thinking skills.

The Greenhaven Literary Companion Series was created with these goals in mind. Designed for young adults, this unique anthology series provides an engaging and comprehensive introduction to literary analysis and criticism. The essays included in the Literary Companion Series are chosen for their accessibility to a young adult audience and are expertly edited in consideration of both the reading and comprehension levels of this audience. In addition, each essay is introduced by a concise summation that presents the contributing writer's main themes and insights. Every anthology in the Literary Companion Series contains a varied selection of critical essays that cover a wide time span and express diverse views. Wherever possible, primary sources are represented through excerpts from authors' notebooks, letters, and journals and through contemporary criticism.

Each title in the Literary Companion Series pays careful consideration to the historical context of the particular author or literary work. In-depth biographies and detailed chronologies reveal important aspects of authors' lives and emphasize the historical events and social milieu that influenced their writings. To facilitate further research, every anthology includes primary and secondary source bibliographies of articles and/or books selected for their suitability for young adults. These engaging features make the Greenhaven Literary Companion series ideal for introducing students to literary analysis in the classroom or as a library resource for young adults researching the world's great authors and literature.

Exceptional in its focus on young adults, the Greenhaven Literary Companion Series strives to present literary criticism in a compelling and accessible format. Every title in the series is intended to spark readers' interest in leading American and world authors, to help them broaden their understanding of literature, and to encourage them to formulate their own analyses of the literary works that they read. It is the editors' hope that young adult readers will find these anthologies to be true companions in their study of literature.

INTRODUCTION

Readings on Arthur Miller offers students a collection of critical essays that are readable, manageable in length, and focused on ideas appropriate to an introductory literary study. The essays and reviews selected for this literary companion cover a wide range of views and interpretations of Miller's key works. They provide insights into the playwright's personal life, his artistic philosophy, his contribution to the history of American drama, and the nature of his themes, characters, and dramatic techniques. This overview of Miller as dramatist presents students with a wealth of material for writing reports, designing oral presentations, or enriching their understanding of one of America's most influential and widely produced playwrights.

Readings on Arthur Miller is organized into five chapters. The first chapter includes articles that provide background on Miller as a writer: early artistic influences, his creative process, his approach to writing, and significant life experiences that have shaped his art. The second chapter focuses on major themes in Miller's work. Chapters three and four assess and analyze Miller's two most notable plays, *Death of a Salesman* and *The Crucible*. Articles focus on specific themes, characterization, and artistic style that make these two plays important to the body of American drama. The essays highlight the basic philosophical underpinnings of his work, key ideas that emerge in his plays, and techniques that characterize his writing style. Chapter five considers some of Miller's other works. Briefly covered are Miller's non-theatrical writings and his first successful play, *All My Sons*.

Other parts of this book offer pertinent material about Miller's life and work. The biographical sketch includes early influences on Miller, important figures in his life, and experiences that shaped his view of society and his art. The chronology outlines a handy overview of Miller's works and places them in a historical time frame. This is supported by a chronological listing of the playwright's works. The bibliography of works identifies valuable resources for students who want to study more about Arthur Miller: his life, his writing, and his place in American theater history.

Arthur Miller's writing career has been punctuated with periods of high praise and harsh criticism. From his first play as a student at the University of Michigan in 1936 to his screenplay for *The Crucible* in 1996, Miller consistently challenges his audiences to look honestly at themselves. The playwright examines the role of the individual, the influence of family and society, and the underlying forces that connect people to their world. This book organizes a meaningful exploration of Arthur Miller's ideas and workmanship.

ARTHUR MILLER: A BIOGRAPHY

The major turning point in Arthur Miller's career occurred when his most critically celebrated play, *Death of a Salesman*, opened on Broadway in February 1949. The production of *Death of a Salesman* transformed Miller's life. The play won the Pulitzer Prize, the Antoinette Perry (Tony) Award, and the Drama Critics' Circle Award. Its success brought Miller fame, critical praise, and substantial wealth. Heralded as one of America's most promising young playwrights, Miller secured his fame after more than ten years of artistic struggle.

Few artists achieve their goals as substantially as Arthur Miller did. But despite his success, Miller continues to question his achievements. His concern for the common man and his distrust of society's institutions often make him feel guilty and uncomfortable with his celebrity. He fears that he will no longer be able to write about the poor when he himself is rich, or that perhaps the trappings of fame will separate him from the essential feelings and insights that generated a play like *Death of a Salesman*. In his autobiography, *Timebends: A Life*, Miller writes, "I was not the first to experience the guilt of success (which, incidentally, was reinforced by leftist egalitarian convictions), and though I suspected the truth, I was unable to do much about it." For Arthur Miller, the struggle to write is a struggle to learn about himself, understand his role as a writer in society, and maintain his idealism, integrity, and political views against popular opinion and criticism.

MILLER'S CHILDHOOD

Born on October 17, 1915, in New York City, Arthur Asher Miller grew up in a middle-class household on 112th Street in Manhattan with his older brother, Kermit, younger sister, Joan, and parents, Isidore and Augusta Miller. His father, an Austrian immigrant, was, for most of Arthur's youth, a successful manufacturer of ladies' coats. Isidore, like many practical-minded immigrant Jews, entered the garment business when he came to New York City in the late 1800s. Arthur's mother, a schoolteacher before she married Isidore, was a conscientious parent who taught her children the customs and heritage of Judaism. Augusta was an avid reader who, according to Miller, could begin a book in the afternoon, finish it by midnight, and recall its details years later. Since no one in the family but Augusta was a reader, she hired a Columbia University student for two dollars a week to discuss novels with her. Augusta was a bright, sensitive woman who was pressed by Miller's grandfathers into marriage within months of graduating with honors from high school. When she told her children the story of her arranged marriage, Miller remembers that her look would suddenly "blacken as she clenched her jaws in anger. 'Like a cow!' she would mutter." In *Timebends: A Life*, Miller suggests that his mother was a "woman haunted by a world she could not reach out to, by books she would not get to read, concerts she would not get to attend, and above all, interesting people she'd never get to meet."

Arthur lived a comfortable middle-class life until age fourteen. It was at this time, in the early stages of the Great Depression, that the family's garment business failed. The loss of the business in 1928 put a great strain on the Millers: Isidore became depressed, both Kermit and Arthur had to take jobs, and the family was forced to move out of their house. As an adolescent, Arthur was deeply disappointed by his father's inability to cope with the loss: "My father simply went more deeply silent, and his naps grew longer, and his mouth seemed to dry up. I could not avoid awareness of my mother's anger at his waning powers." Arthur was also disillusioned with the economic system that put his family in their new predicament; he grew suspicious of the powers that controlled the wealth and the social machinery of society. Later Miller wrote that the depression made him aware that life was often a struggle against powerful social forces outside of the family.

With the loss of their business, the Millers moved to Brooklyn to be near relatives. Arthur attended James Madison High School, where he was actively involved in football and other sports, not unlike Biff Loman in *Death of a Salesman*. Miller focused on staying in good physical shape and improving his athletic skills, not his studies. His friends were athletes, not intellectuals.

After high school, Miller applied to the University of Michigan, but was rejected because his grades were too low. To earn money, he took odd jobs, including a brief stint in the garment business doing various low-level tasks. It was here that he witnessed firsthand how salesmen were often brusquely dismissed or ordered about by insensitive buyers and employers. Later, of course, Miller would create the most famous salesman in literature, Willy Loman. In 1932 Miller began to read simply to occupy his mind between jobs. He read voraciously, particularly Russian writers Fyodor Dostoyevsky and Leo Tolstoy. His discovery of the power of literature sparked his dream of becoming a writer.

MILLER'S COLLEGE YEARS

After several rejected applications, Miller was finally admitted to the University of Michigan in 1934, where he studied journalism, economics, and history. His broad range of study made him skeptical that any one discipline or institution had a monopoly on truth. As a sensitive young college student, Miller began a quest to understand how society changed, how it influenced the individual, and how it could be improved. Miller was attracted to the ideals of socialism—especially its concern for the rights and dignity of the common person. Exhilarated by the prospect of a new social order built on reason, Miller and his fellow student socialists expected "a socialist evolution of the planet" that would bestow a "new and just system." Although his enthusiasm for socialism eventually diminished, many of the liberal political and social ideals he formed in college stayed with him throughout his writing career.

In his junior year, Miller entered a college playwriting contest and, to his surprise, won the first prize of $250. His play *No Villain*, whose characters are modeled on Miller's own family members, deals with the tension within a garment manufacturing family during a bitter labor strike. In *No Villain*, Miller introduces many of the themes and conflicts that dominate his later and more artistic works: the tension between selfishness and humanitarianism, class struggle, conflicts between family members, and the healing bond of family loyalty. Encouraged by the praise of *No Villain*, Miller decided to dedicate himself to writing drama.

Miller graduated from college in 1938 with a degree in English and subsequently supported himself by writing for the Federal Theater Project, a government-sponsored program promoting American writers. While with the project, Miller and fellow Michigan graduate Norman Rosten coauthored *Listen My Children*, an uninspired comedy. The Federal Theater Project did not last long, however: The recently established House Un-American Activities Committee (HUAC) suspected the program of infiltration by communists and abolished it. With the project closed, Miller not only lost his twenty-two-dollar weekly salary, he was also introduced to the harsh tactics of HUAC. Sixteen years later, in 1956, Miller encountered HUAC again when the committee suspected him of subversive behavior and subpoenaed him to defend his social and political views.

MILLER'S EARLY WORK

In 1940 Miller married his sweetheart from the University of Michigan, Mary Slattery. Mary, daughter of an insurance salesman, was a bright student who, according to Miller, had more faith in his ability to write than he had himself. Although she was not actively religious, she was reared a Catholic, and at the time of their marriage both sets of parents were concerned about the intermarriage of a Jew and a gentile. Although the religious conflict in their extended family was disconcerting, Miller and his young wife believed that they could rise about the "parochial narrowness of mind, prejudices, racism, and the irrational" that they felt the tension represented. The couple had two children, Robert and Jane. During World War II, Mary worked as a secretary and Arthur, unable to participate in military service because of a nagging football injury, worked on ships in the Brooklyn Navy Yard and wrote radio plays for the Columbia Broadcasting System. Despite the fact that script writing turned out to be rather lucrative (approximately one hundred dollars a script), Miller hated writing for radio; he chafed under the restrictions and limitations imposed by the radio networks and advertisers and became increasingly suspicious of mixing commercialism and the arts. Nevertheless, as the radio scripts demanded crisp writing and tight organization, this work helped the young playwright refine his craft.

Miller received his first theatrical break in 1944 when *The*

Man Who Had All the Luck was staged on Broadway. The play explores the roles of fate, luck, success, and failure in one's life. Unfortunately, it was not well received by critics and closed after only six performances. In his autobiography Miller says of this play that "standing at the back of the house during the single performance I could bear to watch, I could blame nobody. All I knew was that the whole thing was a well-meant botch, like music played on the wrong instruments in a false scale." Although this play and his other early dramas were unsuccessful, Miller was learning what it took to write a meaningful play. He developed an ear for dialogue and he learned the craft of staging dramas, the needs of actors, and the demands of an audience. Success was not far away.

The Man Who Had All the Luck lost a great deal of money and Miller, now in debt, felt pressured to write his next project, a novel entitled *Focus*. The story's main character is a non-Jew named Lawrence Newman who, after he begins to wear glasses, is mistaken for a Jew. Lawrence is shocked and outraged when he encounters senseless prejudice and anti-Semitism. The novel met with moderate success and was published in England, France, Germany, and Italy. As a Jew himself, Miller experienced only limited encounters with anti-Semitism as a child, but once he began working after high school he was shocked at the extent and intensity of anti-Semitism in America. Because of his own anti-Semitic experiences and following revelations of the Holocaust, Miller committed himself to a lifelong fight opposing anti-Semitism.

MILLER'S FIRST DRAMATIC SUCCESS

At age thirty a frustrated Miller, faced with meager respect and success as a dramatist, decided to give playwriting one last try. Based on an incidental comment by his wife's mother about a young girl who turned in her father to the FBI for manufacturing faulty aircraft parts, Miller began a two-year task of diligently writing and rewriting the play *All My Sons*. He had decided that if he was going to fail as a writer, he would go out with the best possible script. In 1947 this realistic social drama was co-produced by stage and film director Elia Kazan, who at the time was well known but not yet famous. Kazan helped Miller focus and polish the work.

All My Sons follows a thematic pattern Miller established in *Focus*. As the play opens, the audience perceives an atmosphere of normality, a world that is calm, orderly, and peaceful. This placid world is disrupted as the play progresses and the characters expose the audience to a world of tension and disillusionment. The intent of the play is to reveal truths about family, moral decision making, and the role of the individual in society. Although it received mixed reviews, *All My Sons* was widely popular with theatergoers and enjoyed a profitable run of 328 performances. It won the Drama Critics' Circle Award and provided Miller with the renewed energy and resources to press on in his career. On the heels of its Broadway success, in 1948 *All My Sons* was made into a movie starring Edward G. Robinson and Burt Lancaster.

Reflecting on this period of his life, Miller recalls conflicting emotions. On one hand he was proud of his success, but on the other hand he experienced some awkwardness: "As a success I was occasionally greeted by people on the street with a glazed expression that was pleasant but made me feel unnervingly artificial. My identification with life's failures was being menaced by my fame." Miller's reactions aside, with *All My Sons* his status as a playwright was established.

MILLER'S MASTER DRAMA

With the money he earned from *All My Sons*, Miller bought a modest farm in Roxbury, Connecticut. On a knoll by a woods, Miller built a small cabin to which he could escape and write undisturbed. He notes that while he was building he had but two lines for his next play, based on a salesman he had known when he worked for his father: "Willy!" and "It's all right. I came back." Early one morning, sitting in his completed studio, he started writing and by the morning of the next day he had written half a play, which he called *Inside Your Head*. Producers Walter Fried and Kermit Bloomgarden liked the play immediately and convinced Kazan to direct it. With extensive rewriting, the play opened in February 1949 with a new name—*Death of a Salesman*.

Death of a Salesman premiered in Philadelphia to glowing reviews. In his autobiography, Miller tells of his experience watching the first performance. At play's end the audience did not applaud. Instead, they sat in stunned silence, stood up, put their coats on, and sat down again, not wanting to leave the theater. Some people were crying. Finally, almost as an afterthought, the applause exploded. From Philadelphia the production moved to the Morosco Theater on Broadway where it played to packed houses and overwhelming approval. *Death of a Salesman* ran for 742 performances before it closed on November 18, 1950, having won the Drama Critics' Circle Award and the Pulitzer Prize. On its Broadway premiere, Miller became famous. Again, Miller reveals in his autobiography that he struggled with his success. Reflecting on the glory of the first night after the New York opening, with rave reviews flowing from all the critics, Miller writes, "I had striven all my life to win this night, and it was here, and I was this celebrated man who had amazingly little to do with me, or I with him. . . . My dreams of many years had become too damned real, and the reality was less than the dream."

POLITICAL ACTIVITY AND *THE CRUCIBLE*

In the late 1940s and into the 1950s, the cold war between the Soviet Union and the United States, accompanied by a superpower arms race, created an international mood of suspicion and fear. Political, social, and business leaders were increasingly concerned that communism threatened the "American way of life." This so-called Red Scare often bordered on paranoia. It was a tense era, when federal workers were required to take loyalty oaths to pledge their allegiance to America and the government established loyalty boards to investigate reports of communist sympathizers. In 1950 Wisconsin senator Joseph McCarthy and the House Un-American Activities Committee, established to uncover subversive infiltration into American life, turned their anticommunist attention to Hollywood and the intellectual community.

In April 1952, HUAC called Miller's director, Elia Kazan, to testify about communist activity in the theater and motion picture business. He was asked to name individuals who he knew had been members of communist groups, and Kazan named Miller. Both Kazan and Miller were liberals, who, like many intellectuals and artists, dabbled with leftist ideas and causes. Arthur Miller had attended a few meetings of Communist Writers of New York, had signed a petition that protested the banning of the Communist Party, and had been named in a 1947 issue of the *Daily Worker*, a socialist newspaper. Moreover, during the war years, Miller was intrigued by Marxism and had attended some Marxist study courses. Because of his economic troubles during the depression, Miller felt he had experienced the Marxist struggle of the worker against the employer. In *Timebends: A Life* Miller writes that "the concept of a classless society had a disarming sweetness that called forth the generosity of youth. The true condition of man, it seemed, was the complete opposite of the competitive system that I had assumed was normal, with all its mutual hatreds and conniving." But despite the fact that Miller supported left-wing causes, he was not a Communist Party member or sympathizer. After Kazan, HUAC targeted Miller.

Miller was finally subpoenaed to appear before HUAC in 1956. Unlike his friend Kazan, Miller refused to name names. The committee members were unimpressed with the playwright's explanation of artistic freedom and cited Miller for contempt of Congress. Although Miller was found guilty by an overwhelming vote of 373 to 9, public support for his openness and honesty resulted in a reconsideration of his case. In 1958 the U.S. Court of Appeals for the District of Columbia reversed Miller's conviction, stating that he was not informed adequately of the risks involved in incurring contempt.

Miller's response to this anticommunist fear, guilt, and hysteria was *The Crucible*. In 1952 he studied at the Historical Society of Salem (Massachusetts) to draw parallels between the Salem witch trials of 1692 and the twentieth-century Red Scare. The metaphorical play opened on Broadway in 1953 for a decent run of 197 performances. The staging received mixed reviews, but what disappointed the author more than the critical reception of the play was the hostility of the audience. In *Timebends: A Life* Miller writes that "as the theme of the play was revealed, an invisible sheet of ice formed over their heads, thick enough to skate on. In the lobby at the end, people with whom I had some fairly close professional acquaintanceships passed me by as though I were invisible."

As the Red Scare waned, the popularity of *The Crucible* grew. The play had very successful off-Broadway productions in 1954, 1956, and 1965; it was dramatized on television with George C. Scott as John Proctor; and today it is

Miller's most frequently produced play. Modern audiences, long past the McCarthy paranoia, enjoy the universal themes that the drama embodies.

MILLER'S LIFE WITH MARILYN MONROE

By 1951 Mary and Arthur's marriage was beginning to deteriorate, perhaps under the demands of a successful writing career or the pressures of celebrity, or perhaps because Elia Kazan had by then introduced Miller to Marilyn Monroe. Miller comments in *Timebends: A Life* that "when we shook hands the shock of her body's motion sped through me, a sensation at odds with her sadness amid all this glamour and technology." At one point Miller characterized the actress as "the golden girl who was like champagne on the screen." Although they had an occasional correspondence, they did not pursue a serious relationship until 1954, when Monroe divorced her husband Joe DiMaggio, one of the most famous baseball players of his era, and moved to New York City.

The next two years were tumultuous for Arthur Miller. In September 1955 two of Miller's one-act plays, *A View from the Bridge* and *A Memory of Two Mondays*, opened at the Coronet Theater in New York to disappointing and discouraging reviews. In June of that year Miller had contracted with the New York City Youth Board to write a screenplay, but when the project was announced reporter Frederick Woltman viciously attacked Miller for his leftist political views in the *New York Herald-Tribune*. The newspaper article and pressure from the paper's management forced the Youth Board to cancel Miller's film project.

In the early months of 1956, Miller divorced Mary Grace Slattery. Soon after the divorce, in the midst of his political battles with HUAC, Miller made the surprise announcement that he and Marilyn Monroe had been secretly married in a Jewish ceremony (only seventeen days after his divorce). Marilyn had just completed filming the movie *Bus Stop*, and, troubled by personal problems, looked forward to a stable life with Miller. The newspapers minutely and voraciously scrutinized the marriage. Marilyn was depicted as a volatile, sexy bombshell and Miller was pictured as a self-sufficient, intellectual writer. The contrast in personalities, the publicity, and the pressures that both were feeling at the time virtually guaranteed that the marriage would suffer.

Throughout the course of their marriage, Miller's writing fell into a slump. Life with Marilyn consumed him; her need for attention, her mood swings, and her reliance on alcohol and drugs required inordinate amounts of Miller's energy. Miller did manage to adapt his short story "The Misfits," which was first published in *Esquire* in 1957, into a screenplay specifically for Marilyn. The movie *The Misfits*, directed by John Huston, was filmed in Nevada with Montgomery Clift, Clark Gable, and Marilyn in the pivotal role of Roslyn. During the filming, Marilyn, haunted by depression and drugs, broke down and required time to recuperate in the hospital. By this time the marriage was close to failure. In his autobiography Miller states that Marilyn, confused about who she was, "wanted everything, but one thing contradicted another; physical admiration threatened to devalue her person, yet she became anxious if her appearance was ignored."

The Misfits was first released in 1961 and met with moderate success. That year Marilyn filed for a Mexican divorce and Miller's mother died. For the next twelve months, Miller kept a low profile, publishing only two short stories, "Please Don't Kill Anything" and "The Prophecy." When Marilyn committed suicide with an overdose of sleeping pills in 1962, Miller refused to attend her funeral because he believed the publicity would turn her tragedy into a "circus." The playwright remained silent.

MILLER IN THE 1960s

During the filming of *The Misfits*, Miller met the woman who would become his third wife, Ingeborg (Inge) Morath. Inge, a Vienna-born photographer, was on the film set to take rehearsal photographs. The daughter of research chemists, Inge was educated in Berlin and worked for a while as the Austrian bureau chief for the magazine *Heute.* Both Marilyn and Arthur liked Inge. Miller was immediately attracted to her independence, her strength of character, and her talent as a photographer. Marilyn Monroe also gravitated to her because of the photographer's kindness and nonaggressive attitude. Marilyn particularly appreciated the fact that Inge portrayed her with great affection and sensitivity. At a time when Miller was obsessed with his failing marriage and his stalled writing career, Inge's confidence and stability must have been very appealing.

Despite Miller's resolve never to marry again, just over a year after his divorce from Monroe, Miller and Morath married in February 1962, six months before Monroe's suicide on August 5. Arthur and Inge would have a daughter, Rebecca, eighteen months later. Miller was extremely happy with Inge, but he was struggling to find the inspiration to write again. The Millers spent most of their time at Roxbury. Here, Miller worked on his next play, *After the Fall*, his first in nine years. *After the Fall* opened in 1964 at the ANTA Theater–Washington Square. Swamped by preproduction publicity, the play was hyped in the media as not only the reemergence of a great playwright but also a play about Marilyn Monroe. *After the Fall* suffered some of the worst criticism that Miller had ever received. Many critics accused Miller of overusing obvious autobiographical details and shamelessly exploiting his relationship with the popular actress. The main character, Quentin, appears to be Miller himself and the character Maggie, who dies of an overdose of sleeping pills, recalls the recently deceased Monroe. Miller argues that the harsh criticism was inevitable: "I was soon widely hated, but the play had spoken the truth as, after all, it was obliged to do, and if the truth was clothed in pain, perhaps it was important for the audience to confront it uncomfortably and even in the anger of denial." *After the Fall* incorporates the despair of *The Misfits* and contains some of the familiar Miller themes of guilt, self-deception, and the quest for meaning.

Despite the controversy, *After the Fall* played to large audiences and Miller was encouraged by his producers to write another. His new play, *Incident at Vichy*, was written in a very short time and opened in 1964, again to reviews that were generally unfavorable. Based on the story of an analyst friend, Dr. Rudolph Loewenstein, who hid from the Nazis in Vichy France in 1942, the play attacks anti-Semitism. Interestingly, *Incident at Vichy* was not produced in France because of the fear that audiences might resent the implication that the French cooperated with the Nazi attack on the Jews.

MILLER'S FIGHT FOR ARTISTIC FREEDOM

In the mid-1960s Miller's plays were often staged before large audiences in Europe, where the playwright was very popular. As a result, Miller spent a good deal of time in Europe viewing and helping present his work. While in Paris in 1965, Miller was encouraged to become the next president of PEN, an international writers' organization of poets, playwrights, editors, essayists, and novelists. PEN was established after World War I by writers including Bernard Shaw and H.G. Wells to help fight censorship and champion the freedom of writers. Miller was skeptical at first, but after a few days of reflection he agreed to serve as its new leader. Having accepted the responsibility of the PEN presidency, he realized that "willy-nilly, I was pitched into the still indeterminate tangle of detente politics to begin a new and totally unexpected stage of my learning life."

As the head of PEN for the next four years, Miller dedicated himself to uplifting the social and political status of writers. Miller believed that PEN must serve as the conscience of the world's writing community. Perhaps his dedication to this task stemmed from his treatment by HUAC, where the playwright learned firsthand that writers are often trapped by political pressures. As did many organizations after World War II, PEN operated with a cold war mentality that made it uncompromisingly anti-Soviet. In the sixties, as relations with Eastern Europe were being reexamined, PEN was finally making some attempts to enlist and support Soviet writers. As president, Miller convinced a Soviet delegation, headed by the Russian writer Alexei Surkov, to join the international organization.

Miller's dedication to PEN and the writers it represented is exemplified by the fact that Miller delivered a scheduled speech at the opening of the New York PEN Congress in 1966 despite the fact that his father died that day. Miller found the strength to deliver the speech because he was convinced that PEN was the one organization that could apply leverage to protect the rights of writers internationally. Before he retired as PEN president in 1969, Miller urged governments around the world to release writers who were imprisoned for political reasons, particularly in Lithuania, South Africa, Czechoslovakia, Latin America, and the Soviet Union.

In 1968 Miller resumed playwriting with *The Price*, a work about two brothers who cannot overcome their anger with each other. Reminiscent of his earlier work, *The Price* probes family relationships, suffocating illusions, and the power of the past to influence the present. The original staging of the

play was beset by problems that troubled Miller. The director and actors were caught in a battle of artistic and egotisti-
cal differences, the lead performer dropped out because of
illness, and the playwright himself was eventually enlisted
to direct the play during the week before it opened on Broadway at the Morosco Theater. Despite its problems, the play
opened to cordial but generally unenthusiastic reviews and
ran for 425 performances. At the same time *The Price*
opened, Viking Press, Miller's publisher, awarded the playwright a gold title page of *Death of a Salesman* to honor the
sale of one million copies. This honor emphasizes the fact
that despite the mixed reviews that Miller often received, his
audience deeply appreciates the power of his work.

MILLER'S POLITICAL ACTIVISM

Professionally rejuvenated by the success of *The Price*, Miller
carried his influence into the arena of politics. Dismayed by
the 1963 assassination of President John Kennedy, racial inequality, poverty, and the escalating U.S. involvement in
Vietnam, Miller accepted the nomination by his fellow Roxbury, Connecticut, Democrats to attend the 1968 Chicago
Democratic National Convention as their delegate. Miller
went to Chicago to support peace activist Eugene McCarthy
and to introduce a resolution on the floor of the convention
to cease U.S. bombing in Vietnam. When his resolution was
rejected, Miller wrote that he "felt totally defeated by the absence of any spoken word commemorating the long fight to
end the war, and by the abdication of the men who had led
the struggle within the Democratic Party and were now allowing it to vanish . . . unmourned and unsung." The convention itself turned chaotic and the antiwar protests outside
the convention hall turned violent as the Chicago police
clashed with protesters. This experience seemed to cap
Miller's fear that values in America were breaking down, violence was becoming epidemic, and government was acting
with increased paranoia and force.

Reflecting on his political activism in *Timebends: A Life*,
the playwright states that "the sixties was a time of stalemate
for me. . . . I could find no refreshing current of history such
as I had imagined touching in the thirties and forties, only a
moral stagnation that mocked creation itself." Nevertheless,
Miller reaffirmed his need to write social drama because,
despite the chaos of the age, the common people "still

wanted better lives for their kids, wished marriages could last, and clung to a certain biological decency."

MILLER IN THE 1970s

In the 1970s Miller wrote three plays: *The Creation of the World and Other Business* (1972), *The American Clock* (1976), and *The Archbishop's Ceiling* (1977). The productions of all three works were harshly criticized. *The Creation of the World and Other Business* closed after only twenty performances; *The Archbishop's Ceiling* had a short life at Washington's Kennedy Center. However, like a delayed reaction, both *The American Clock* and *The Archbishop's Ceiling* found a receptive audience in London during the mid-1980s.

Throughout the 1970s Miller continued to fight tirelessly for the rights of individuals and the freedom of writers. For example, he helped free Brazilian writer Augusto Boal, imprisoned for his political beliefs. In 1972 Miller publicly criticized the three-year sentence given to publisher Ralph Ginzburg for an obscenity conviction that was appealed all the way to the U.S. Supreme Court. Because of a letter to Miller from famous Czech poet and playwright Pavel Kohout, Miller organized fifty-three other writers and literary figures to sign a written statement sent to the Czech leaders protesting their arrest of dissident thinkers. Miller was a major voice in the process to free dissident Russian writer Aleksandr Solzhenitsyn, whose moral strength Miller had compared to that of John Proctor in *The Crucible*. For his effort, the Soviet government banned all of Miller's works. The irony was not lost on Miller, who pointed out that his plays had been under attack by his own government for his suspected communist sympathies and that now the Soviet government had banned his work for pushing American-style individual rights.

Perhaps the best example of Miller's involvement in the struggle of the individual against governmental authority is found in the case of Peter Reilly, who was convicted of brutally slashing his mother's throat in Canaan, Connecticut, in 1973. The case came to Miller's attention two years later when he read the transcript of Reilly's interrogation. Miller, like the friends and neighbors of the Reilly family, felt that the police had methodically and cynically broken the will of the exhausted and frightened young Peter and forced him to sign a confession. Miller enlisted the help of a lawyer friend and a private investigator to reopen the case, bring about a new trial, and ultimately free Peter Reilly. The Reilly case was a perfect cause for the playwright who had for so long concerned himself with individual rights, the abuse of authority, the perplexing nature of truth, and the themes of justice and morality. The Reilly case also reflects Miller's fascination with the law. To the playwright, who includes a lawyer in almost all of his plays, the law is the last defense against society's inability to see or accept the truth. Reflecting on the case in his autobiography, Miller writes, "If the long months of the Reilly case left a darkened picture of man, it was no less perplexing for being accompanied by the most unlikely examples of courage and goodness, of people rising to the occasion when there was little reason to expect they would."

MILLER'S REVIVAL IN THE 1980S

During the eighties Arthur Miller's works experienced a worldwide revival. Shortly after *A View from the Bridge* opened on Broadway in 1983, Miller and his wife traveled to Beijing, China, to see a production of *Death of a Salesman*. In Beijing the audience responded positively to the elementary human concerns dramatically portrayed in *Death of a Salesman*. Miller writes in his autobiography that "the Chinese reaction to my Beijing production of *Salesman* would confirm what had become more and more obvious over the decades in the play's hundreds of productions throughout the world: Willy was representative everywhere, in every kind of system, of ourselves in this time."

In 1984 the revival continued on Broadway with the opening of *Death of a Salesman* starring Dustin Hoffman as Willy Loman. Dustin Hoffman also played the lead in the 1985 CBS televised production of the play, which was broadcast to an audience of more than twenty-five million viewers. In addition, *The Price* was successfully revived on Broadway and in 1989 *The Crucible*, directed by Arvin Brown, was staged in New Haven. America was beginning to understand Arthur Miller's contribution to American theater, art, and consciousness. This recognition of his long and prolific career climaxed when Miller won the Kennedy Center Honors award for distinguished lifetime achievement in 1984. At the award banquet a powerful irony struck the playwright; the ceremony was held in the same room in which Miller faced the House Un-American Activities Committee almost thirty years earlier.

CONCLUSION

Miller's most recent plays have not enjoyed successful theatrical runs. In 1991 his play *The Ride Down Mt. Morgan* premiered in London, but ran for only three months. His latest play, *The Last Yankee,* a comedy-drama, also suffered a short life span after it opened in 1993 at the Manhattan Theatre Club in New York. Now in his eighties, Miller is still working. He recently completed a screenplay for a 1996 movie version of *The Crucible,* starring Winona Ryder as Abigail.

In his autobiography, it is apparent that the experiences of Miller's life have merged with his artistic goals to create a very personal body of work. The impact of his family, the depression, his discovery of drama at the University of Michigan, his unfortunate standoff with HUAC, his marriages, his political activism as president of PEN, his protest of the war in Vietnam, and his ongoing relationship with the theater, its critics, and its audiences have all coalesced to shape the form and power of his plays.

The characters in Miller's dramas act out human concerns that engage the playwright personally. He calls on his characters to take responsibility for their actions, and Miller himself never shies away from his responsibility to act on his own convictions. Miller rejects self-pity in his characters, and he consistently rebounds from harsh criticism. Miller wants his characters to find the strength to overcome moral paralysis and act on the world, and Miller sticks to his moral beliefs against popular opinion. In a sense Miller is similar to Ben in *Death of a Salesman*—he went into the "jungle" and came out a success; he did not succumb to the nullifying illusions that defeated Willy Loman. He carried on a dialogue with himself, his family, and his audience that continues to this day. Miller lives with his wife Inge at the same home in Roxbury, Connecticut, that he purchased after the success of *All My Sons.* He is a grandfather to his son's three children; his two daughters, Rebecca and Jane, are both involved in the arts; and his wife's love of photography continues.

Throughout his career, Miller's works reveal the idea that beneath the chaos of reality there are hidden forces that connect all human beings to one another and to the world. It is with this major theme that Miller chooses to end his autobiography. Pondering the coyotes that he can see outside his Roxbury studio window, Miller writes, "I am a mystery to them until they tire of it and move on, but the truth, the first truth, probably, is that we are all connected, watching one another." As thousands of audiences watch the interior workings of Arthur Miller unfold on stage, the playwright moves them to wonder about that truth.

CHAPTER 1

A General Introduction to the Playwright

READINGS ON
ARTHUR MILLER

An Interview with Arthur Miller

Christopher Bigsby

Many of Arthur Miller's plays explore the influences of family, father/son relationships, and the pressures of society. In this interview with drama critic Christopher Bigsby, Arthur Miller talks about his relationship with parents who were in many ways opposites, the world of business, the stock market crash of 1929, the Great Depression of the 1930s, and the economic pressures on his family during his childhood. The playwright discusses how the attitudes he took on in childhood find their way into his plays.

Christopher Bigsby is a professor and senior lecturer in American literature at the University of East Anglia, Norwich, England. His major works include *Confrontation and Commitment: A Study of Contemporary American Drama: 1959–66* and *Miller on File.*

Bigsby: Am I right in sensing a gulf between your parents: your mother, on the one hand, committed to culture, actually hiring a student to read novels to her; and your father, much more committed to the material world, and, indeed, barely literate.

Miller: That's right, there was a cultural space between them, and as I went on I made much of it because a kid growing up needs to learn to read, he needs to learn to absorb the culture that is given him, and my father could be of no help there. He was barely able to read and write and so I naturally gravitated towards my mother for that. But, as time went on, I found he had a certain taste which was basically mine, much more than hers. She was very sentimental about books, about people, about everything; he was far more realistic, in a peasant-like way. Some idea had to operate; he had no intellectual pretensions whatsoever, so just having an idea was

From *Arthur Miller and Company*, edited by Christopher Bigsby (London: Methuen, 1990). Copyright ©1990 by The Arthur Miller Centre for American Studies. Reprinted by permission of Reed Consumer Books Ltd.

no great thing for him. He wanted to know what happened as a result of it, where did it lead, how did it change anything. Fundamentally he was on the right track. So I was caught between the two of them and I think it was fruitful. . . .

Bigsby: The very first play you wrote when you were a student at the University of Michigan was in some ways about your family, and your father emerges from that a rather bewildered man, certainly not in tune with what then would have been called progressive forces. He was a decent man but in a way a failure. I notice that in your autobiography you list a number of American writers whose fathers were failures or whose sons regarded them as failures. Would you place yourself in that category?

Miller: I certainly would. That was the ethos that I grew up with in fact; it was the standard operating procedure. I think it may still be. One rarely hears of an American writer, I don't know about England or Europe, whose father was to be regarded as, in any way, adequate or successful. The writer in America is supplanting somebody, correcting him, making up for his errors or failures, and in the process he is creating a new world. He is the power that the father had lost. . . .

Oddly enough I've noticed that in a number of Chinese stories and novels there are an enormous number of stories about fathers who are gradually losing their marbles and their authority. And then the Crash, of course, had a tremendous impact because I was so convinced of the authority of the system that I lived in and in which my father was a great success. That success had flowed over on to him, so that when the actual physical crash came what it took with it was the authority of anybody who claimed authority. . . .

THE WORLD OF BUSINESS

Bigsby: What was your response to the business world. Did it shape you in any way?

Miller: Well, through these experiences I learned a lot about it from the underbelly. These were small businesses that were highly competitive and in a Depression period which made it even worse. I had, I guess, a torn attitude about it. On the one hand, I shared the mores of business, that is that you had to work hard and keep your nose clean and if you succeeded it was good and if you failed it wasn't. On the other hand, the scale of values always bothered me a lot. I usually got involved with the failures in the place, of which I concede myself to be one, the people who didn't fit in this scheme of things, including a lot of salesmen who passed through, and they always moved me very much. Some of them were very sensitive, intelligent men who were simply scrapped. It was by nobody's will. It was really a dog eat dog situation, much more so than today, probably, excepting maybe on the highest levels of industry where they cut each other's throats on principle; but down below, there, it was a rough place for anybody to work and I found myself thrown in with a lot of these men from time to time.

THE STOCK MARKET CRASH OF 1929

Bigsby: You were what, fourteen, when the Crash came?

Miller: Yes.

Bigsby: What sort of impact did that have on your life and your family's life?

Miller: It was revolutionary. I remember I was playing handball on the street one day against a wall of the building and some fellow was playing with us. He was older than I was. He was already at University somewhere. And he started to tell me that the reason the Depression had occurred was because the workers hadn't been paid as much as they should have been and they couldn't buy back what had been produced. It was a Marxist argument. I remember standing there and thinking, everything is upside down. Of course I'd been brought up to think that workers belonged where they were. The reason they were workers was that they couldn't get to be bosses. Therefore it was always better to be the boss than the worker because the boss represented the end of your striving, your perfection, and the worker was a state of imperfection. So that day I recall very clearly thinking, 'My God, the whole thing is upside down. I should be wanting to be a worker.' You see. Anyway, it was revolutionary in all different ways. You suddenly realised that the great leaders of society were full of hot air. The thing was built on smoke. There were really no underpinnings. The head of the Stock Exchange had landed in prison for seven years for some crookedness. Certainly you had to believe in the banks, but they were closing up all over the place.

THE IMPACT OF THE CRASH ON MILLER'S FAMILY

Bigsby: What happened to your own family?

Miller: Oh, they were ruined by it, just destroyed by it and very quickly. It was a story that was repeated millions of times in the United States on a larger scale than ours but it was big enough. My father had a business that probably employed eight hundred to a thousand people. It was one of the largest coat companies in the United States and in a period of, I don't know, probably a year or so, there was absolutely nothing left of it. The bottom dropped out of the whole thing. People forget, you know, that the American Banking Association went to Franklin Roosevelt and asked him to nationalise the banks. That came from the bankers. It was simply out of control. They didn't think they could bring back any kind of a usable banking system. So if they were talking about nationalising banks, you can imagine what we were talking about. When it first happened, people imagined the this would pass in a few weeks. After all the Stock Market had gone up and down a few times. But it kept going down and when they said it was all over, it kept going down again. Pretty soon nothing was worth anything and the effect on us, my family, was tremendous because, like a lot of other people, my father had realised, some time in the early or middle 20s, that while he had a perfectly lucrative business manufacturing women's coats, he could make immeasurably more money on the Stock Market than anybody could ever make in a business. So, like a lot of other businessmen, he put more and more capital into the Stock Market. And things were great for about four years until 1929–30 when the bottom fell out of it. So, in short order, like a lot of other people, he lost his capital and he lost a perfectly viable business which, had he not gambled with capital, would probably have survived. And the country went into hock. That is, everybody was in debt, whether it be for their home or their business or whatever, and the banks found it impossible to collect on the loans that they had made because people had lost what they had borrowed and the banks began to fail. I remember very clearly the time when I was on my bicycle passing a bank that I passed a thousand times on my way to school and there was a crowd of people out front and a policeman standing in front of the closed gates of that bank. It was about eleven o'clock in the morning. The policeman was explaining what had happened to their money. You can imagine the desperation involved in asking a policeman to describe what had happened to their money. And he, of course, was as bewildered as anybody. There was simply no

Governmental regulation to catch the falling bodies. These people could go nowhere. Suddenly, of one morning, they had no assets. They couldn't buy food. They had what was in their pockets or what was in a drawer in the house. So the structure of the world shook. This big heavy looking bank turned out to be a fraud. What could you believe in, then? One banker after another on Monday would make a statement that everything was going to be all right and on Thursday he had jumped out of a window. So, within about six months of the Crash, I would say, possibly a little longer, you were naked on the beach. There was nothing to lean on. There was no security anywhere. The country was a fraud. It stunned my parents at first and then my father went back and tried to start a new business. He borrowed money from some place or another. He was now going into business in a period of Depression when the unemployment was something like twenty per cent after a while, that was the countable unemployed. There was no purchasing power so no business could survive then and he never recovered in his whole lifetime. Everybody was scrabbling around for any kind of a job. I went to work delivering bread and rolls at four thirty in the morning before I went to high school. I got four dollars a week for about twenty five hours. I was fortunate, I thought, to get this job. Four dollars sounds like a ridiculous sum, and it was, but you could buy a quart of milk for eight cents and, later on, I could buy some smoking tobacco for nine cents or something.

FATHER AND THE CRASH

Bigsby: It occurs to me that it must have been almost a double blow to your father, because surely, in a sense, it was a blow to his manhood. That's to say, his status was being attacked. When you were a teenager and presumably of an age to challenge his status anyway, did it make relationships between the two of you difficult?

Miller: It didn't make them overtly difficult. I had great pity for him. Somewhere in my head I knew that it was not his responsibility that this had happened. However, he thought it was his responsibility. That was a distinctive thing about the American Depression of the 30s. The people blamed themselves, not the system, by and large, which is why the country never got radicalised in any way. They didn't blame the system. On the whole there was more self-blame than anything else. And it therefore became my job in effect to teach him that he should stop blaming himself so much. I did that because I slowly became more and more Marxist as the thing went on, as did my whole generation to one degree or another, because it was the only viable explanation, as you could imagine, for this whole thing having happened. We were not accustomed, in those days, to think of the thing as a system anyway. I never heard the word used, frankly—the word 'system'. You weren't in the system. You were in some sort of a free arena where each person went out to test himself. And that didn't change, of course. We are still in that arena, many of us. I went into my life not expecting any help from anywhere. I was amazed when the Government started to create programmes where you helped the people somehow. You expected people to get knocked off, destroyed, by bad luck. Then you either had to become entirely cynical about the whole world, which I was not set up to do, or you had to get busy creating a new one so that that creation of the new one and the rejection of absolute cynicism has really been the theme of much of my work. I'm not a fatalist. I don't believe there is no hope for man, but I do believe we stand on a very thin edge and that it is liable to go down at any moment. It was interesting in the late 80s, with the Stock Market on the slide again, to listen to a replay of the same speeches that were being made in 1929. Ronald Reagan announced that it was just an adjustment. That's like saying that the collision of two major planets is an adjustment of the universe. And it was some of what the hated Roosevelt put in place in the great hundred days after he got into office which prevented the unravelling of the whole sweater, though of course no one was going to admit that. Had we had the free economy, that we are all of course in favour of, we would all have been in the drink by now. But we don't have a free economy. We haven't had one at least since 1934, thank God, and the result was that you could stop these haemorrhages by certain measures that were put in then. . . .

MILLER SUMS UP THE 1930s

Bigsby: What's the most acute memory you have of that period that in some way sums up the 30s and the Depression to you.

Miller: Endless, boundless waiting. The 30s have been

characterised as a time of great struggle, which they were in the sense that our trade unions were formed then, or re-formed, and the country became conscious of the Government's obligation to extend help in various ways, but any neighbourhood you went into was full of grown people with nothing to do. That's where I grew up. Grown men were playing football in the streets in the middle of the work-day, living with in-laws, and the conversations were about how somebody had hit it rich somehow or somebody had sung a song and gotten on the radio and made twenty-five dollars. Everything was about money, you see. This was obsessional. Where was the next dollar going to come from. It's almost impossible to imagine any more a country with no public as-sistance. You see, people were living on each other. There were six-roomed houses with eighteen people living in them, tripping over each other to go to the one bathroom, all related and all calling themselves middle-class people. They might even have a car. The absurdities of it all were what hit you. It was a dusty time and the summers were the most dreadful time of all for a young guy because you had gone through school and thought that in the fall you would go back to school and the point arrived where school was com-ing up and you weren't going back. What do you do all those October/November/December days? That was what was dreadful. Everything was put off. Whatever you thought of was greeted with a sigh that maybe someday one could do that again, but not soon. It was agony, especially in a coun-try where in all our memories, even mine, you thought you could pretty much do what you thought you wanted to do.

Miller's Writing Process

Allan Seager

Allan Seager explains that behind the polished plays of Arthur Miller is an artistic struggle replete with creative stops and starts, failures and successes, strategies and luck. Seager looks at the stages of Miller's writing process: the origins of his plays, the early drafts, the development of characters, the emergence of the drama as a thematic whole, and the eventual staging of the play.

Allan Seager was a professor of English at the University of Michigan, Ann Arbor. His work includes the novels *Amos Berry* and *Death of Anger*. He also wrote a biography of Theodore Roethke and published more than eighty stories in various magazines. Seager and Miller were close friends.

Not long ago Arthur Miller was called by Kermit Bloomgarden, the producer, who asked him when he would have his next play ready. Show business is flourishing. Theatres are hard to find and Bloomgarden wanted to make sure he could rent one, not for the 1959 but for the 1960 season. Miller replied, "I don't know. I'm working on it, but I can't tell yet." Miller's answer indicates an area of knowledge that is usually blank or mysterious to the public, that is, just what Miller does when he "works" on a play. Theatregoers are impressed by the play they see. Critics quite properly can pronounce only on the finished work. They are concerned with the results of the playwright's art rather than with the art itself, one of whose chief elements is sheer stamina, and because they are so seldom described, few people are aware of the myriad of patient individual insights, the barren pauses, the earnest, even desperate stratagems, the lucky breaks, and the compromises that finally take shape as the play they see.

The play Miller is now working on ran, at one time, to two reams of paper typewritten. This comes to about a thousand

Allan Seager, "The Creative Agony of Arthur Miller," *Esquire*, October 1959, pp. 123-36. Reprinted by permission of Joan Seager Fry.

pages; a finished play script is about a hundred and twenty. These pages were covered with dialogue, but it lacked the succinctness, the concentrated meaning, in fact, the poetry of dramatic speech. Miller was merely letting his characters talk, giving them their heads to say anything that might be remotely relevant to his purposes for them, not that these purposes were yet entirely clear. But after all this effort, the play did not come together and Miller got fed up. He dumped the two reams of paper into the wastebasket and they were taken out and burned. A waste? Hardly, for after a thousand pages of talk he knew his characters almost as well as he knows his friends. However, the work was at a standstill and Miller could not see how to give it the next push.

Familiar as they were by this time, the characters and principal actions were recalcitrant. Try as he would Miller could not bring up the one intuition that would make the play a whole, make it, in effect, a play he could work on. Miller knows his craft and he realized it was time to stop trying. "Inspiration" is a word that has been blunted by high-school English teachers talking about the Romantic poets, but it was inspiration he was waiting for. This is not a gratuitous *éclaircissement;*[1] it is the result of work, and, although you can toss a manuscript into the wastebasket, you can't toss it out of your head so easily. Miller turned his attention to other things among them the script of *The Misfits*, a movie John Huston is making with Marilyn Monroe, but the gists and themes of the work he had already done gathered weight and meaning in some unworried subliminal part of his mind until one day, abruptly, he had the crucial insight. It lay in the phrase, "to lay a hand on life." To explain why this phrase was essential or where its efficacy lay would probably require an impossibly minute history of the life and times of Arthur Miller, and the timing of the flash might elude even that. It was enough that the block was demolished and he could go to work again.

THE ORIGINS OF A PLAY

Miller says that work on a play is a "discovery of meaning," simultaneously the definition of a theme and its significance, but the theme of a play is not necessarily in its germ, its first beginning. Miller starts, not with any attempt to form

1. sudden illumination

a theme, but merely with something that interests him. This seems obvious enough, yet Flaubert[2] wrote a great novel about the story of the Delamarre family which, he complained, did not interest him in the least. Literary psychologists have devoted a good deal of study to this phenomenon of interest, not much of it very fruitful. Excited laymen are always coming to writers with "a wonderful story you can use" and are disappointed when the writer remains listless, uninterested, in fact. What touches off Miller's interest may be a person, a human situation, a phrase, and he may not know why it does at the time. ("I want to make my plays out of evident truths," he says, but this kind of truth usually lies at the end of his labors, not the beginning.)

For instance, the origin of *All My Sons* seems clear and plausible because it adumbrates the major action of the play. It came out of an idle conversation with one of Miller's in-laws, who told of a woman in her neighborhood who turned in her own father for having shipped faulty materials to the government during the war. "The action astounded me," Miller said. "An absolute response to a moral command." Astonishment guarantees interest.

The Origin of *Death of a Salesman*

The beginnings of *Death of a Salesman* are more obscure, more difficult to explain. Miller was at work one night on another play. It was a warm evening in May and suddenly the character of the man who was to become Willy Loman drifted into his head, a memory of a man he had known. The accretion of ideas and emotions around this figure seemed to be instantaneous, and Miller wrote two-thirds of the first draft that night; the last third took him three months. After the play was running on Broadway, Miller was looking for something in his files and happened to find an old manuscript of a play he had begun at the University of Michigan about the same man. He had completely forgotten about it, but the man, a salesman in his life had apparently gone on working in his head, unconsciously gathering the force that made the play come easily, and that the play released.

"What I am working for is the gasp," Miller says. "I used to stand at the back of the theatre when *Death of a Salesman* was playing and hear it." For a while after the play opened,

2. French novelist Gustave

he got phone calls and telegrams from salesmen saying things like this: "I saw your play. I've just quit my job. What do I do now?" Two large corporations asked him to address their sales meetings. The total meaning of the play is not simple, but Miller felt he had been successful by his own standards when the salesmen themselves were struck so sharply by it. One salesman, as he was leaving the theatre, was overheard to say: "I always said that New England territory was no damned good."

THE ORIGIN OF *THE CRUCIBLE*

The origins of *The Crucible* lay back in Miller's college years also. He had been fascinated then by the Salem witch trials, but they did not seem to be the stuff of a play until the McCarthy hysteria brought the story back to his mind and he noticed similarities. At this point, Miller had no play in mind, only the possibility of one. He went to the courthouse in Salem and said, "I'd like to see the record of some trials that took place here several years back." The clerk said, "Just when would that be?" "About 1695," Miller said. With unshakable aplomb, the clerk laid the big hand-written folios of the witch trials in front of him and he began to study them.

His decision to write a play out of them did not come, however, until he found that John Proctor was being mysteriously spared by Abigail Williams, who was clearly trying to hang his wife, and when it came out that Abigail had been the Proctors' servant girl. Miller says, "The pettiness of the inner reality compared to the perverse grandeur of the social paroxysm made a great impression. It was like my own situation then—trying to tell people that the great 'issues' which the hysteria was allegedly about were covers for petty ambitions, hardheaded political drives, and the fantasies of very small and vengeful minds. Equally, I imposed the theme of Proctor's handing over his conscience to his wife and taking it back again with the resolve that he was good enough to hang. I felt that people in our time did not think themselves good enough to fight, were too privately guilty to withstand the accusations of guilt that were coming down daily from government and press." Once he had a beginning, Miller took many lines of the play directly from the court records.

These are the germs of three plays. The people and the situation or the people *in* the situation compelled his attention. Their actions excited him; that is, they interested him. It is doubtful whether he or any writer analyzes further at this stage. Objectively it is clear that the starting points of *All My Sons* and *The Crucible* were moral decisions of the highest seriousness, that one was topical and the other analogous to a contemporary situation, and that these starting points were discovered, not invented. . . .

MILLER'S WRITING PROCESS

Miller has two places to work. One is a fourteen-by-fourteen split-shingle cabin behind his house at Roxbury, Connecticut. During the cold weather he customarily uses the cabin on weekends. (The first winter he tried to heat it with a stone fireplace, but the cabin was set wrong and the chimney wouldn't draw. Now he has a space heater and can write in comfort.) In the summer he's there for weeks at a time. The other place is an office in his apartment. It is a plainly furnished workroom with a desk, a sofa, a couple of chairs, a wall of books, and his files. The view from the single window is not of the Golfe-Juan or the ocean at Big Sur; it is merely uptown New York, and his desk faces away from it anyway. When Miller looks up he sees two beautiful photographs of his wife[3] which, to many people, might be more distracting than the view from any window whatever. But they are perhaps less so to Miller, who has only to stick his head out of the door and call to see the original.

What goes on in these rooms? What does Miller do when he works? Assuming that he has the germinal person or incident with him when he enters, he begins with notebooks. These are ordinary dime-store spiral notebooks. He does not sit down and fill the notebooks, writing smoothly like a clerk for five or six hours a day. He writes as things occur to him (with pauses for thought or reading in between), spasmodically, chaotically, with pen or pencil, (he has no preference): aphorisms, scraps of dialogue invented or recalled, short or long poems left incomplete, drawings of sets for as-yet-unconceived plays, personal memoranda in which he talks to himself or asks himself the meaning of some dream or childhood incident, spurts of plotting which may suddenly reveal a whole act, or, with luck, the beginning, middle and end of a play. Here, at random, are some samples:

M. You ought to pay more attention to your wife.

3. at the time, Marilyn Monroe

D. That's all I do. I never knew you had to cultivate a wife until recently.

M. Well, you don't just plant them and let them grow by themselves.

D. Tells of his unhappiness.

Then. . . .

I. God! Who would ever have believed I would need sixty thousand dollars a year to live! And I'm not even living.

Then. . . .

Beware following the details to the loss of vision.

Then. . . .

Beware following the vision to the loss of details.

Then. . . .

It is first of all *ironic.* A man devoting his whole effort to avoiding a certain kind of disaster and discovering that it happened to him at the moment he changed his course to avoid it—the disaster was his challenge, the life that he never lived.

Then. . . .

S believes we are all living with an image of someone we are intent on deceiving—either by pretending to be like him or by trying to show hatred where there is only unrequited love. Deception is his *structure.*

Then. . . .

His question: Should he have adopted such a life?

My question: Did he really *adopt* anything?

Then. . . .

Remember the nature of his work. Remember pity. The erosion of the tentative commitment to a particular job for sixteen years.

Then. . . .

He calls her *perceptive.* It means she sees through him. He respects and fears her, therefore. . . .

During the early stages, "work" is the setting down of notes like these, reminders of thinking. Some of them might be called permanent observations on his craft applicable to any play, but most of them have a connection, however tenuous, with the theme, the over-all idea, he is trying to elucidate. And the little decision as to whether a given note is worth putting down, whether it is relevant or not, helps define what it is relevant *to,* that is, the play he is trying to get to emerge as a whole.

All the time he is taking these notes by hand, Miller will

be writing scenes on the typewriter, "believing on certain mornings that the time is ripe to drive directly toward the stage," but, again, "such false dawns can go on for months."

These successive acts of creation have little to do with logical thought. For weeks at a time, Miller's attention may be fixed on some character's face or on the feeling of revelation some experience has left behind. It is very hard to put one's feet on the desk (Miller is a long, gangling man and tends to do this) and merely think, day after day. The attention is slippery. These jottings, although most of them will be thrown away, fend off the devils of distraction and inertia that beset every writer. One other, a private devil of Miller's own, is a facility: "I could always write a good scene," he says, "but not always *the* scene," and he has to guard against false starts.

When the play begins to take shape in his mind at last, suddenly the aphorisms will disappear, the poems, the drawings, and there will be a whole notebook with nothing in it but dialogue and structural notes. Miller works at these until, again with luck and after no telling how long a time, the moment comes "when thinking is left behind. Everything is in the present tense and a play emerges which has resemblances but little else to the mass of notes left behind." It is, or it is similar to, an organic process, and comparisons with the bud and the flower or the chrysalis and the butterfly are obvious.

Miller sees his work as a constant effort to penetrate to a core of meaning in his material, a center of rich significance—a significance which has its own strict order: A dramatic order that he feels with all its nuances rather than an intellectual statement of meaning which could be summarized, say, in an essay. "There are two questions I ask myself over and over when I'm working, 'What do I mean? What am I trying to say?'" he says, but this meaning could not be contained in a flat linear statement or in an actor's lines, his pauses, or his gestures. The speeches and gestures are only implements. Ideally, the meaning lies in the minds of the man or woman in the audience, and the play in its entirety reveals it to them.

A finished script lying on a desk is still no more a play than the score of a symphony is the music. Both must be performed. Between Miller's desk and the rising of the curtain there are the producer, the director, the scene designer, and the actors. "From the time I finish the writing until the first performance, everything is a compromise," he says. . . .

Each director has his strengths and weaknesses and these must be balanced against the qualities of the script. There is one director who can handle scenes of physical action brilliantly, evoking almost a shimmer of meaning from the composition of the simplest movements. Another, by his reticence, can pull astonishing performances from actors, make them play over their heads. Another is personally so unpopular that, Miller says, "There are people in this town who, if this man came into their offices, would call the police," but he is fantastically conscientious and he has had a great many hits. The play must suit the director's peculiar talents for, ultimately, no matter how long and patiently he and Miller work together, it is the director's vision of the play that reaches the stage.

MILLER COMMENTS ON THE CRITICS

In his autobiography, Timebends: A Life, *Arthur Miller defends his work against wide negative critical reception.*

But *After the Fall*'s reception was not as uniformly negative as I imagined in the heat of the moment. When I looked back, it was obvious that aside from *Death of a Salesman* every one of my plays had originally met with a majority of bad, indifferent, or sneering notices. Except for Brooks Atkinson at the beginning, and later Harold Clurman, I exist as a playwright without a major reviewer in my corner. It has been primarily actors and directors who have kept my work before the public, which indeed has reciprocated with its support. Only abroad and in some American places outside New York has criticism embraced my plays. I have often rescued a sense of reality by recalling Chekhov's remark: "If I had listened to the critics I'd have died drunk in the gutter."

After the director, the scene designer must be selected. Each one naturally can do one kind of thing better than another. One's strong point may be the construction of a striking set; another can evoke the mood of the script through his lighting. "A set should be a metaphor of the whole play. For instance, the set of MacLeish's[4] *J.B.* looks somewhat like a circus tent, but at the same time it suggests the whole world as the scene of Job's trials. It's very effective," Miller says.

4. American poet Archibald

While he is writing, Miller has learned not to visualize the scene of the dramatic action too definitely. Any good scene designer must obviously be left room to develop his own conceptions and if Miller approached him with the sets rigidly erected in his own mind, the designer's freedom would be lost. "I had some notions about the set of *Death of a Salesman,* but when I saw Jo Mielziner's sketches for the set and his ideas about the lighting, I knew they were better than anything I had imagined," Miller says. A concession like that is easy to make, but it demonstrates that the stage performance is clearly not the flower of the playwright's efforts alone.

CASTING THE PLAY

Miller has never yet written a part with a particular actor in mind. He is present at all tryouts. An example of the kind of compromise casting demands can be seen in the choosing of an actor to play Willy Loman. Writing the play, Miller had taken it for granted that Willy was a little guy, and at first several small men, among them Ernest Truex, tried out for Miller and Elia Kazan, the director. However, Lee J. Cobb, a large man, was very anxious to get the part and he flew his own plane from Hollywood to New York three times to read for Willy Loman. The brilliance of his trial performances so impressed Miller and Kazan that Cobb was hired and, in the memories of most playgoers today, he *is* Willy Loman. Once an actor has been selected and rehearsed, he must be given some leeway in interpreting his part, but this trust has its dangers. An actor in one of Miller's plays had been doing a superb job during the first weeks of the run. His performances showed great tact and a personal flair that heightened the impact the play was making. Miller and the director congratulated themselves for having picked him for the role, but one day the actor casually asked Miller a question which revealed that he understood neither his own part, its relation to the play, nor the play as a whole. Miller was almost afraid to answer, for fear he would let some light into a splendid darkness of the actor's conception. But Miller did answer cautiously and the actor continued his fine work. It is enough to freeze the blood.

Rehearsals last three-and-a-half to four weeks and it is then, in the darkened theatre with his feet up on the seat in front of him, that Miller puts in the twelve-hour day and, maybe, after sending out for coffee, fourteen. Then the final touches are given to the interpretation, the pace, the nuances of gesture, the timing of exits and entrances. There is always the line some actor cannot possibly say that must be rewritten. There is the piece of business that must somehow be made to come off now because the dates are fixed for the out-of-town tryout and the New York opening. And as the tension mounts Miller's responsibility for his play lessens until on opening night it rests with the actors alone.

After the opening, what happens to the play depends on the critics and the public. If neither like it, it fails, obviously. If both do, it is a hit and there is a barrel of money in a hit. Investors have to wait until the play is off the nut before they make any profits, but the playwright's returns begin when the curtain goes up. . . .

Yet there is not an artist now living who has made fewer concessions to box-office standards than has Arthur Miller. It is not that he has a mission, a word that suggests nutfooders and end-of-the-world guys with whiskers; rather he has an aim. "The playwright's function," he says, "is to tell the people what goes on." Leaving out such implications as the question, "Why don't they already know, considering all their sources of information?" and omitting such words as "commitment," and "engage," which have already been used about Miller and his work many times, it is possible to derive the meaning of this statement. What goes on is not good, as any of his plays will show. Miller's anxiety is spent in the gap between man as he is and man as he could be. (That it is *man*, and not people from Brooklyn or Americans, is clear from the success of his plays abroad.) Miller is perhaps less ready to believe than he once was that this gap can be narrowed by the passage of wise laws, the election of competent officials, or any organized gestures whatever. He is thinking more closely on man's lack of any profound concern with his own true nature and his consequent failure to recognize the true nature of his inevitable bonds with others. What goes on, in short, is a failure of love.

Miller said recently in conversation, "Writing a play is so damned tough that, when I finish one, I swear I'll never write anything again, not even a letter." He has recovered from this exhaustion every time, however, and it is practically certain that Kermit Bloomgarden can go ahead and rent a theatre for the 1960 season.

Influences on Miller's Writing

Arthur Miller

In a speech delivered in 1958, Arthur Miller discusses what has influenced his writing. Miller states that the depression of the 1930s shaped his view of reality. He points to Fyodor Dostoyevsky, Eugene O'Neill, and Henrik Ibsen as models of the premise that a writer must not only tell the story of his characters as they relate to the world, but that he must also reveal the hidden forces beneath the chaos of reality that tie the characters together.

Arthur Miller is an American playwright, novelist, and short story writer. His Pulitzer Prize–winning drama *Death of a Salesman* and his widely produced play *The Crucible* make Miller one of America's most influential dramatists of the modern period.

I see by the papers that I am going to talk today on the subject of the literary influences on my work. It is probably a good subject, but it isn't what Harold Clurman[1] and I discussed when he asked if I would speak here. What he had in mind was something else. I am supposed to widen your horizons by telling something about the frame of reference I used when I started to write, and that included books I read, or music I heard, or whatnot.

I doubt whether anybody can widen horizons by making a speech. It is possible, perhaps, by writing a play. Still, I may be able to suggest an approach to our theater which—even if it is not valid for everyone—will not be quite the same as that of the various critics; and if nothing else is accomplished here maybe it will at least appear that there is another way of looking at drama.

1. literary critic

Tolstoy wrote a book called *What Is Art?* The substance of it is that almost all the novels, plays, operas, and paintings were not art but vanity, and that the rhythm with which a Russian peasant swung a scythe was more artful than all the dance on Moscow stages, and the paintings of peasants on the sides of their wagons more genuine than all the paintings in the museums. The thing that disheartened him most, I believe, was that inevitably artistic creation became a profession, and the artist who may have originated as a natural quickly became self-conscious and exploited his own gifts for money, prestige, or just for want of an honest profession.

Yet, Tolstoy went on writing. The truth, I suppose, is that soon or late we are doomed to know what we are doing, and we may as well accept it as a fact when it comes. But the self-knowledge of professionalism develops only as a result of having repeated the same themes in different plays. And for a whole theater the time for self-appraisal comes in the same way. We are, I believe, at the end of a period. Certain things have been repeated sufficiently for one to speak of limitations which have to be recognized if our theater is not to become absurd, repetitious, and decayed.

THE INFLUENCE OF THE DEPRESSION

Now one can no sooner speak of limitations than the question of standards arises. What seems like a limitation to one man may be an area as wide as the world to another. My standard, my viewpoint, whether it appears arbitrary, or true and inevitable, did not spring out of my head unshaped by any outside force. I began writing plays in the midst of what Allan Seager, an English teacher friend of mine at Michigan, calls one of the two genuinely national catastrophes in American history—the Great Depression of the 'thirties. The other was the Civil War. It is almost bad manners to talk about depression these days, but through no fault or effort of mine it was the ground upon which I learned to stand.

There are a thousand things to say about that time but maybe one will be evocative enough. Until 1929 I thought things were pretty solid. Specifically, I thought—like most Americans—that somebody was in charge. I didn't know exactly who it was, but it was probably a business man, and he was a realist, a no-nonsense fellow, practical, honest, responsible. In 1929 he jumped out of the window. It was bewildering. His banks closed and refused to open again, and

I had twelve dollars in one of them. More precisely, I happened to have withdrawn my twelve dollars to buy a racing bike a friend of mine was bored with, and the next day the Bank of the United States closed. I rode by and saw the crowds of people standing at the brass gates. Their money was inside! And they couldn't get it. And they would never get it. As for me, I felt I had the thing licked.

But about a week later I went into the house to get a glass of milk and when I came out my bike was gone. Stolen. It must have taught me a lesson. Nobody could escape that disaster.

I did not read many books in those days. The depression was my book. Years later I could put together what in those days were only feelings, sensations, impressions. There was the sense that everything had dried up. Some plague of invisible grasshoppers was eating money before you could get your hands on it. You had to be a Ph.D. to get a job in Macy's. Lawyers were selling ties. Everybody was trying to sell something to everybody else. A past president of the Stock Exchange was sent to jail for misappropriating trust funds. They were looking for runaway financiers all over Europe and South America. Practically everything that had been said and done up to 1929 turned out to be a fake. It turns out that there had never been anybody in charge.

What the time gave me, I think now, was a sense of an invisible world. A reality had been secretly accumulating its climax according to its hidden laws to explode illusion at the proper time. In that sense 1929 was our Greek year. The gods had spoken, the gods whose wisdom had been set aside or distorted by a civilization that was to go onward and upward on speculation, gambling, graft, and the dog eating the dog. Before the crash I thought "Society" meant the rich people in the Social Register. After the crash it meant the constant visits of strange men who knocked on our door pleading for a chance to wash the windows, and some of them fainted on the back porch from hunger. In Brooklyn, New York. In the light of weekday afternoons.

I read books after I was seventeen, but already, for good or ill, I was not patient with every kind of literature. I did not believe, even then, that you could tell about a man without telling about the world he was living in, what he did for a living, what he was like not only at home or in bed but on the job. I remember now reading novels and wondering, What do these people do for a living? When do they work? I remember asking the same questions about the few plays I saw. The hidden laws of fate lurked not only in the characters of people, but equally if not more imperiously in the world beyond the family parlor. Out there were the big gods, the ones whose disfavor could turn a proud and prosperous and dignified man into a frightened shell of a man whatever he thought of himself, and whatever he decided or didn't decide to do.

THE LESSON OF THE DEPRESSION

So that by force of circumstance I came early and unawares to be fascinated by sheer process itself. How things connected. How the native personality of a man was changed by his world, and the harder question, how he could in turn change his world. It was not academic. It was not even a literary or a dramatic question at first. It was the practical problem of what to believe in order to proceed with life. For instance, should one admire success—for there were successful people even then. Or should one always see through it as an illusion which only existed to be blown up, and its owner destroyed and humiliated. Was success immoral?— when everybody else in the neighborhood not only had no Buick but no breakfast? What to believe?

An adolescent must feel he is on the side of justice. That is how human indignation is constantly renewed. But how hard it was to feel justly, let alone to think justly. There were people in the neighborhood saying that it had all happened because the workers had not gotten paid enough to buy what they had produced, and that the solution was to have Socialism, which would not steal their wages any more the way the bosses did and brought on this depression. It was a wonderful thought with which I nearly drove my grandfather crazy. The trouble with it was that he and my father and most of the men I loved would have to be destroyed.

Enough of that. I am getting at only one thought. You can't understand anything unless you understand its relations to its context. It was necessary to feel beyond the edges of things. That much, for good or ill, the Great Depression taught me. It made me impatient with anything, including art, which pretends that it can exist for its own sake and still be of any prophetic importance. A thing becomes beautiful to me as it becomes internally and externally organic. It becomes beautiful because it promises to remove some of my helplessness before the chaos of experience. I think one of the reasons I became a playwright was that in dramatic form everything must be openly organic, deeply organized, articulated from a living center. I used long ago to keep a book in which I would talk to myself. One of the aphorisms I wrote was, "The structure of a play is always the story of how the birds came home to roost." The hidden will be unveiled; the inner laws of reality will announce themselves; I was defining my impression of 1929 as well as dramatic structure.

THE INFLUENCE OF DOSTOYEVSKY

When I was still in high school and ignorant, a book came into my hands, God knows how, *The Brothers Karamazov*. It must have been too rainy that day to play ball. I began reading it thinking it was a detective story. I have always blessed Dostoyevsky for writing in a way that any fool could understand. The book, of course, has no connection with the depression. Yet it became closer, more intimate to me, despite the Russian names, than the papers I read every day. I never thought to ask why, then. I think now it was because of the father and son conflict, but something more. It is always probing beyond its particular scenes and characters for the hidden laws, for the place where the gods ruminate and decide, for the rock upon which one may stand without illusion, a free man. Yet the characters appear liberated from any systematic causation.

The same yearning I felt all day for some connection with a hidden logic was the yearning in this book. It gave me no answers but it showed that I was not the only one who was full of this kind of questioning, for I did not believe—and could not after 1929—in the reality I saw with my eyes. There was an invisible world of cause and effect, mysterious, full of surprises, implacable in its course. The book said to me: "There is a hidden order in the world. There is only one reason to live. It is to discover its nature. The good are those who do this. The evil say that there is nothing beyond the face of the world, the surface of reality. Man will only find peace when he learns to live humanly, in conformity to those laws which decree his human nature."

THE INFLUENCE OF IBSEN AND O'NEILL

Only slightly less ignorant, I read Ibsen in college. Later I heard that I had been reading problem plays. I didn't know what that meant. I was told they were about social problems, like the inequality of women. The women I knew about had not been even slightly unequal; I saw no such problem in *A Doll's House*. I connected with Ibsen not because he wrote about problems, but because he was illuminating process. Nothing in his plays exists for itself, not a smart line, not a gesture that can be isolated. It was breath-taking.

From his work—read again and again with new wonders cropping up each time—as well as through Dostoyevsky's, I came to an idea of what a writer was supposed to be. These two issued the license, so to speak, the only legitimate one I could conceive, for presuming to write at all. One had the right to write because other people needed news of the inner world, and if they went too long without such news they would go mad with the chaos of their lives. With the greatest of presumption I conceived that the great writer was the destroyer of chaos, a man privy to the councils of the hidden gods who administer the hidden laws that bind us all and destroy us if we do not know them. And chaos, for one thing, was life lived oblivious of history.

As time went on, a lot of time, it became clear to me that I was not only reporting to others but to myself first and foremost. I wrote not only to find a way into the world but to hold it away from me so that sheer, senseless events would not devour me.

I read the Greeks and the German Expressionists at the same time and quite by accident. I was struck by the similarity of their dramatic means in one respect—they are designed to present the hidden forces, not the characteristics of the human beings playing out those forces on the stage. I was told that the plays of Aeschylus must be read primarily on a religious level, that they are only lay dramas to us now because we no longer believe. I could not understand this because one did not have to be religious to see in our own disaster the black outlines of a fate that was not human, nor of the heavens either, but something in between. Like the howling of a mob, for instance, which is not a human sound but is nevertheless composed of human voices combining until a metaphysical force of sound is created.

I read O'Neill in those days as I read everything else—looking to see how meaning was achieved. He said something in a press conference which in the context of those years seemed to be a challenge to the social preoccupations of the 'thirties. He said, "I am not interested in the relations of man to man, but of man to God." I thought that very reactionary. Until, after repeated and repeated forays into one play of my own after another, I understood that he meant what I meant, not ideologically but dramatically speaking. I too had a religion, however unwilling I was to be so backward. A religion with no gods but with godlike powers. The powers of economic crisis and political imperatives which had twisted, torn, eroded, and marked everything and everyone I laid eyes on.

I read for a year in economics, discovered my professors dispensing their prejudices which were no better founded than my own; worse yet, an economics that could measure the giant's footsteps but could not look into his eyes.

I read for a year in history, and lost my last illusion on a certain afternoon at two-thirty. In a lecture class a student at question time rose to ask the professor if he thought Hitler would invade Austria. For fifteen minutes the professor, by no means a closet historian but a man of liberal and human interests, proved why it was impossible for Hitler to invade Austria. It seems there were treaties forbidding this which went back to the Congress of Vienna, side agreements older than that, codicils, memoranda, guarantees—and to make a long story short, when we got out at three o'clock there was an extra being hawked. Hitler had invaded Austria. I gave up history. I knew damned well Hitler was going to invade Austria.

In that sense it was a good time to be growing up because nobody else knew anything either. All the rules were nothing but continuations of older rules. The old plays create new plays, and the old histories create new histories. The best you could say of the academic disciplines was that they were breathlessly running after the world. It is when life creates a new play that the theater moves its limbs and wakens from its mesmerized fixation on ordinary reality; when the present is caught and made historic.

I began by speaking of standards. I have labored the point long enough to state it openly. My standard is, to be sure, derived from my life in the 'thirties, but I believe that it is as old as the drama itself and was merely articulated to me in the accent of the 'thirties. I ask of a play, first, the dramatic question, the carpenter-builder's question—What is its ultimate force? How can that force be released? Second, the human question—What is its ultimate relevancy to the survival of the race?

Miller's Questioning by the House Un-American Activities Committee

Sheila Huftel

After World War II and throughout the 1950s, Americans increasingly feared the spread of communism. In an atmosphere of public and private suspicion, the House Un-American Activities Committee, HUAC, was formed to investigate and ultimately identify communist sympathizers. HUAC subpoenaed many artists, actors, and writers to prove that they were not or had not been active in the Communist Party. Much of the evidence working against those who were called amounted to nothing more than hearsay and unwarranted accusations from unreliable witnesses and sources.

Arthur Miller was summoned before HUAC in 1956. The committee wanted the playwright to turn over the names of fellow writers who were present at communist writers' meetings he attended in New York City during the 1940s. Throughout his testimony, Miller makes reference to his work and the needs of a writer. The committee considered Miller's discussion of his art a needless digression and an annoying cover-up. When Miller refused to name others, he was found guilty of contempt, fined five hundred dollars, and given a thirty-day suspended jail sentence. In 1958 the ruling was overturned.

Sheila Huftel was a drama critic for the *Stage*, a British publication. Much of her material in *Arthur Miller: The Burning Glass* came directly from interviews with Arthur Miller.

On Thursday, June 21, 1956, Arthur Miller was summoned to appear before the House Committee on Un-American Activities, where he refused to turn informer and name people he had seen at Communist writers' meetings ten years before. Here are extracts from the "Testimony of Arthur Miller, accompanied by Counsel, Joseph L. Rauh, Jr." The chairman of the Committee was Francis E. Walter; Richard Arens was staff director. It was Part 4 of an "Investigation of the Unauthorized Use of United States passports, 84th Congress.". . .

MR. ARENS: Now, your present application for a passport pending in the Department of State is for the purpose of traveling to England, is that correct?

MR. MILLER: To England, yes.

MR. ARENS: What is the objective?

MR. MILLER: The objective is double. I have a production which is in the talking stage in England of *A View from the Bridge*, and I will be there to be with the woman who will then be my wife.[1] That is my aim.

MR. ARENS: Have you had any difficulty in connection with your play *A View from the Bridge* in its presentation in England?

MR. MILLER: It has not got that far. I have had the censor in England giving us a little trouble, yes, but that is general. A lot of American plays have that difficulty.

REFUSING THE ROLE OF INFORMER

MR. ARENS: Do you know a person by the name of Sue Warren?

MR. MILLER: I couldn't recall at this moment.

MR. ARENS: Do you know or have you known a person by the name of Arnaud D'Usseau? D'-U-s-s-e-a-u?

MR. MILLER: I have met him.

MR. ARENS: What has been the nature of your activity in connection with Arnaud D'Usseau?

MR. MILLER: Just what is the point?

MR. ARENS: Have you been in any Communist Party sessions with Arnaud D'Usseau?

MR. MILLER: I was present at meetings of Communist Party writers in 1947, about five or six meetings.

MR. ARENS: Where were those meetings held?

MR. MILLER: They were held in someone's apartment. I don't know whose it was.

MR. ARENS: Were those closed party meetings?

MR. MILLER: I wouldn't be able to tell you that.

MR. ARENS: Was anyone there who, to your knowledge, was not a Communist?

---

1. actress Marilyn Monroe

MR. MILLER: I wouldn't know that.

MR. ARENS: Have you ever made application for member-ship in the Communist Party?

MR. MILLER: In 1939 I believe it was, or in 1940, I went to attend a Marxist study course in the vacant store open to the street in my neighborhood in Brooklyn. I there signed some form or another.

MR. ARENS: That was an application for membership in the Communist Party, was it not?

MR. MILLER: I would not say that. I am here to tell you what I know.

GILES REFUSES TO NAME HIS INFORMANT

The Crucible, first produced in 1953, concerns innocent people who get caught in a menacing hysteria in which sus-picion, fear, and deviousness replace evidence and truth. The dialogue between the authorities (Hathorne and Danforth) and an accused townsman (Giles) has frightening similarities to the type of questioning that Miller himself faced when he was called before the House Un-American Activities Commit-tee in 1956.

GILES: . . . If Jacobs hangs for a witch he forfeit up his property—that's law! And there is none but Putnam with the coin to buy so great a piece. This man is killing his neigh-bors for their land!

DANFORTH: But proof, sir, proof.

GILES, *pointing at his deposition:* The proof is there! I have it from an honest man who heard Putnam say it! The day his daughter cried out on Jacobs, he said she'd given him a fair gift of land.

HATHORNE: And the name of this man?

GILES, *taken aback:* What name?

HATHORNE: The man that give you this information.

GILES, *hesitates, then:* Why, I—I cannot give you his name.

HATHORNE: And why not?

GILES, *hesitates, then bursts out:* You know well why not! He'll lay in jail if I give his name!

HATHORNE: This is contempt of the court, Mr. Danforth!

DANFORTH, *to avoid that:* You will surely tell us the name.

GILES: I will not give you no name. I mentioned my wife's name once and I'll burn in hell long enough for that. I stand mute.

DANFORTH: In that case, I have no choice but to arrest you for contempt of this court, do you know that?

MR. ARENS: Tell us what you know.

MR. MILLER: This is now sixteen years ago. That is half a lifetime away. I don't recall and I haven't been able to recall and, if I could, I would tell you the exact nature of that application. I understood then that this was to be, as I have said, a study course. I was there for about three or four times perhaps. It was of no interest to me and I didn't return.

MR. ARENS: Who invited you to attend?

MR. MILLER: I wouldn't remember. It was a long time ago.

MR. ARENS: Tell us, if you please, sir, about these meetings with Communist Party writers you said you attended in New York City.

MR. MILLER: I was by then a well-known writer. I had written *All My Sons*, a novel, *Focus*, and a book of reportage about Ernie Pyle and my work with him on attempting to make the picture *The Story of G.I. Joe*. I did the research for that, so that by that time I was quite well known, and I attended these meetings in order to locate my ideas in relation to Marxism because I had been assailed for years by all kinds of interpretations of what Communism was, what Marxism was, and I went there to discover where I stood finally and completely, and I listened and said very little, I think, the four or five times.

COMMITTEE PRESSURE

MR. ARENS: Could I just interject this question so that we have it in the proper chronology? What occasioned your presence? Who invited you there?

MR. MILLER: I couldn't tell you. I don't know.

MR. ARENS: Can you tell us who was there when you walked into the room?

MR. MILLER: Mr. Chairman, I understand the philosophy behind this question and I want you to understand mine. When I say this I want you to understand that I am not protecting the Communists or the Communist Party. I am trying to and I will protect my sense of myself. I could not use the name of another person and bring trouble on him. These were writers, poets, as far as I could see, and the life of a writer, despite what it sometimes seems, is pretty tough. I wouldn't make it any tougher for anybody. I ask you not to ask me that question.

(The witness confers with his counsel.)

I will tell you anything about myself, as I have.

MR. ARENS: These were Communist Party meetings, were they not?

MR. MILLER: I will be perfectly frank with you in anything relating to my activities. I take the responsibility for everything I have ever done, but I cannot take responsibility for another human being.

MR. ARENS: This record shows, does it not, Mr. Miller, that these were Communist Party meetings?

(*The witness confers with his counsel.*)

MR. ARENS: Is that correct?

MR. MILLER: I understood them to be Communist writers who were meeting regularly.

MR. ARENS: Mr. Chairman, I respectfully suggest that the witness be ordered and directed to answer the question as to who it was that he saw at these meetings.

MR. JACKSON: May I say that moral scruples, however laudable, do not constitute legal reason for refusing to answer the question. I certainly endorsed the request for direction.

THE CHAIRMAN: You are directed to answer the question, Mr. Miller.

MR. MILLER: May I confer with my attorney for a moment?

(*The witness confers with his counsel.*)

Mr. Walter, could I ask you to postpone this question until the testimony is completed and you can gauge for yourself?

THE CHAIRMAN: Of course, you can do that, but I understand this is about the end of the hearing.

MR. ARENS: This is about the end of the hearing. We have only a few more questions. The record reflects that this witness has identified these meetings as meetings of the Communist writers. In the jurisdiction of this committee he has been requested to tell this committee who were in attendance at these meetings.

MR. DOYLE: If I understand the record, the record shows that he answered that he did not know whether there were any non-Communists there, or not. I think the record so shows.

MILLER'S WRITING INCOMPATIBLE WITH MARXISM

MR. MILLER: I would like to add, sir, to complete this picture, that I decided in the course of these meetings that I had finally to find out what my views really were in relation to theirs, and I decided that I would write a paper in which, for the first time in my life, I would set forth my views on art, on the relation of art to politics, on the relation of the artist to politics, which are subjects that are very important to me, and I did so and I read this paper to the group and I discovered, as I read it and certainly by the time I had finished with it, that I had no real basis in common either philosophically or, most important to me, as a dramatist. I can't make it too weighty a thing to tell you that the most important thing to me in the world is my work, and I was resolved that, if I found that I was in fact a Marxist, I would declare it; and that, if I did not, I would not declare it and I would say that I was not; and I wrote a paper and I would like to give you the brunt of it so that you may know me.

THE CHAIRMAN: Have you got the paper?

MR. MILLER: I am sorry, sir. I think it is the best essay I ever wrote, and I have never been able to find it in the last two or three years. I wish I could. I would publish it, as I recall it, because it meant so much to me. It was this: That great art like science attempts to see the present remorselessly and truthfully; that, if Marxism is what it claims to be, a science of society, that it must be devoted to the objective facts more than all the philosophies that it attacks as being untruthful; therefore, the first job of a Marxist writer is to tell the truth, and, if the truth is opposed to what he thinks it ought to be, he must still tell it because that is the stretching and the straining that every science and every art that is worth its salt must go through.

I found that there was a dumb silence because it seemed not only that it was non-Marxist, which it was, but that it was a perfectly idealistic position, namely, that, first of all, the artist is capable of seeing the facts, and, secondly, what are you going to do when you see the facts and they are really opposed to the line? The real Marxist writer has to turn those facts around to fit that line. I could never do that. I have not done it.

I want to raise another point here. I wrote a play called *All My Sons* which was attacked as a Communist play. This is an example of something you raised just a little while earlier about the use of my play in the Communist meeting, of a different sketch that I had written. I started that play when the war was on. The Communist line during the war was that capitalists were the salt of the earth just like workers, that there would never be a strike again, that we were going to go hand in hand down the road in the future. I wrote my play called *All My Sons* in the midst of this period, and you probably aren't familiar with it—maybe you are—that the story is the story of an airplane manufacturer, an airplane parts manufacturer, who sends out faulty parts to the Air Force.

Therefore, what happened was that the war ended before I could get the play produced. The play was produced. The Communist line changed back to an attack on capitalists and here I am being praised by the Communist press as having written a perfectly fine Communist play. Had the play opened when it was supposed to have opened; that is, if I could have sold it that fast, it would have been attacked as an anti-Communist play.

The same thing has happened with *Salesman. Death of a Salesman* in New York was condemned by the Communist press.

THE CHAIRMAN: Mr. Miller, what has this to do—

MR. MILLER: I am trying to elucidate my position on the relation of art.

MR. ARENS: Was Arnaud D'Usseau chairman?

MR. SCHERER: Just a minute, Mr. Chairman, may I interrupt?

THE CHAIRMAN: Yes.

MR. SCHERER: There is a question before the witness; namely, to give the names of those individuals who were present at this Communist Party meeting of Communist writers. There is a direction on the part of the chairman to answer that question.

Now, so that the record may be clear, I think we should say to the witness—Witness, would you listen?

MR. MILLER: Yes.

MR. SCHERER: We do not accept the reasons you gave for refusing to answer the question and that it is the opinion of the committee that, if you do not answer the question, that you are placing yourself in contempt.

CHAPTER 2

Major Themes in Miller's Plays

READINGS ON

ARTHUR MILLER

The Domestic Realism of Arthur Miller

Gerald M. Berkowitz

During the first decades of the twentieth century, American dramatists experimented in form and style. America's most innovative playwright, Eugene O'Neill, ultimately established the dominant American dramatic form, called domestic realism. According to Gerald Berkowitz, domestic realism works on the principles that drama should be set in the present, without pretentious attempts at high tragedy or the heroic, and revolve around ordinary people as they deal with personal problems associated with marriage, love, earning a living, making friends, and maintaining a family. Domestic realism proved to be a theatrically adaptable, rich, and enduring dramatic form.

During the 1950s, domestic realism was shaped by the two most influential playwrights of the post–World War II period: Arthur Miller and Tennessee Williams. Williams explored the psychological and spiritual dimension of domestic realism, whereas Miller expanded the dramatic possibilities of the common man.

Gerald Berkowitz teaches in the Department of English at Northern Illinois University, at De Kalb. He has contributed numerous articles to theater journals and magazines. His earlier works include *New Broadway: Theatre Across America* and *The Plays of David Garrick.*

The American drama is, for all practical purposes, the twentieth-century American drama. There were plays written and performed on the American continent well before there was a United States, and during the nineteenth century the American theatre was widespread and active. But, as was also true in much of Europe, it was, with rare exceptions, not the home of a particularly rich or ambitious liter-

From *American Drama of the Twentieth Century* by Gerald M. Berkowitz (New York: Longman, 1992). Copyright © Longman Group UK Ltd., 1992. Reprinted with permission of the publisher.

ature. The theatre was a broadly popular light entertainment form, much like television today; it is possible to do artistically ambitious work on American commercial television, but television is not likely to be the first medium to come to the mind of a serious writer. This is not to say that the playwrights of the nineteenth century were without talent, but that, like television writers, they were more likely to be artisans skilled at producing the entertaining effects that audiences wanted, than artists looking to illuminate the human condition or challenge received values.

Yet in America, as in Europe, a change in the kind of literature being written for the theatre began to become apparent in the last years of the nineteenth century. As with many historical and artistic developments in American culture, this was much less a matter of an organized 'movement' than of trial and error and accidents of personality; an individual writer might not be consciously innovating, but something in his work might attract audiences or inspire other writers, so that the art form lurched forward a step. There is, for example, little evidence that James A. Herne considered *Margaret Fleming* (1890) revolutionary in any way, but with hindsight we can see that his version of the mildly sensational melodrama typical of the period raises moral questions that its contemporaries do not, and that those questions give the play a distinctly twentieth-century feel. The process was slow and unsteady, with false starts and relapses, but by the second decade of the twentieth century artistically ambitious writers were venturing into drama and finding it able to carry a weight of psychological insight and philosophical import it had not been asked to carry before.

THE SEARCH FOR AN AMERICAN DRAMATIC FORM

This was very much a rebirth of an art form; with little in the recent history of the genre to build on, the first generations of twentieth-century American dramatists had to discover for themselves what shape the twentieth-century American drama would take. It is not surprising, then, that the years from say, 1900 to 1930 saw a great variety of dramatic styles and vocabularies, as playwrights experimented with epic, symbolism, expressionism, verse tragedy and the like, finding out as they went along what a play could and could not do. Foremost among the experimenters was Eugene O'Neill, of whom it is only a slight exaggeration to say that during the 1920s he never wrote two plays in the same style. O'Neill, whose father had been a star of the nineteenth-century theatre, and who thus had a sharp awareness of its literary limitations, was consciously experimenting, trying to shape and stretch the medium so it could do what he wanted it to—express his profoundly thought-out insights and philosophies. But even the less determinedly innovative writers of the period found themselves making up the rules as they went along.

DOMESTIC REALISM AS THE VOICE OF AMERICAN DRAMA

Inevitably, some experiments failed. One reason O'Neill kept changing styles was that many of them disappointed him, while some of the "-isms" that were briefly successful in Europe proved unamenable to American topics and tastes, or simply uncommercial. Through trial and error, however, one particular dramatic mode came to the fore. Theatrically effective, easy for audiences to relate and respond to, remarkably flexible in its adaptability to the demands of different authors, the natural voice of American drama was revealed by the 1930s to be in realistic contemporary middle-class domestic melodrama and comedy.

Realistic contemporary middle-class domestic melodrama—each of those words is worth examining and defining. "Realism" does not mean the uncensored photographic and phonographic record of external reality. Dramatic realism is an artifice as much as any other mode, violating reality in order to give the illusion of reality; to take one simple example, characters in "realistic" plays generally speak one at a time, and in grammatical sentences. The important point is that the illusion of reality is maintained; realism avoids gross violations of the laws of nature (People don't fly) or the introduction of purely symbolic characters or events (the Little Formless Fears of O'Neill's *The Emperor Jones*), while presenting characterizations and behaviour that are at least possible. And thus a realistic play asserts the claim that it speaks the truth, that what happens on stage is a reflection of the world its audience inhabits.

Historical plays were a mainstay of the nineteenth-century American drama, and continued to be written in the twentieth; most Broadway seasons in the 1920s saw at least one play about eighteenth-century France or nineteenth-century Mexico, and the 1930s had a thin but constant stream of plays about Washington, Lincoln or other American heroes. But the overwhelming majority of twentieth-century American plays are set in the present, again implying a close parallel to the real world. Moreover, a play set in the here and now is likely to reflect the external reality of the here and now, be it the Depression of the 1930s, the middle-class anxieties of the 1950s or the profound social changes of the 1960s and after; and one of the first important discoveries about domestic realism was that it could address large social and historical issues in theatrical terms.

MILLER TALKS ABOUT TENNESSEE WILLIAMS

Arthur Miller describes in his autobiography, Timebends: A Life, *with a mixture of admiration and competitiveness, his reaction to Tennessee Williams's* A Streetcar Named Desire. *Miller realized all playwrights benefited from Broadway productions of rival works.*

I could not imagine a theatre worth my time that did not want to change the world, anymore than a creative scientist could wish to prove the validity of everything that is already known. I knew only one other writer with the same approach, even if he surrounded his work with a far different aura. This was Tennessee Williams. . . .

When [director Elia] Kazan invited me up to New Haven to see the new Williams play, *A Streetcar Named Desire*—it seemed to me a rather too garishly attention-getting title—I was already feeling a certain amount of envious curiosity since I was still unable to commit myself to the salesman play [*Death of a Salesman*], around which I kept suspiciously circling and sniffing. But at the same time I hoped that *Streetcar* would be good; it was not that I was high-minded but simply that I shared the common assumption of the time that the greater the number of exciting plays there were on Broadway the better for each of us. At least in our minds there was still something approximating a theatre culture to which we more or less pridefully belonged, and the higher its achievement the greater the glory we all shared. The playwright then was king of the hill, not the star actor or director, and certainly not the producer or theatre owner as would later be the case.

Shakespeare wrote about kings, O'Neill wrote about Lazarus and Marco Polo, and Maxwell Anderson wrote about Elizabeth I and Mary of Scotland. But the overwhelming majority of modern American plays are about people from the same social and economic world as the playgoers—the urban middle class. That is not a narrow range, and can stretch from the barely-getting-by and underemployed to the comfortably well-off. But the extremes of the economic ladder, along with other fringes of society—blacks, rustics, etc.—are rarely represented before the 1960s, except as stereotypes, and infrequently thereafter except in plays specifically addressing minority subjects. Audiences for American plays are likely to see themselves or people like them, or people they might believably, with good or bad luck, be like.

Of all these adjectives being defined "domestic" may be the most significant. Not only are American plays about recognizable people in a recognizable world, but they are about the personal lives of these people. Whether a play is actually set in a living room, with a cast made up solely of family members, as an extraordinary number are, or whether the "domestic" setting extends to an office and a circle of friends, the issues and events are presented in small and localized terms. Whatever the deeper meanings of an American play, on one solid level it is about love and marriage, or earning a living, or dealing with a family crisis.

Of course Americans did not invent domestic drama. Ibsen and Chekhov (to name just two) had written of realistic characters in domestic situations, and even hinted at larger social and moral issues through this mode. The gradual discovery of American dramatists, starting in the 1930s, was that domestic realism was their most effective vehicle for talking about larger issues—that the small events in the lives of small people could be presented so that they reflected the world outside the living room. Put another way, the insight becomes more than merely technical. Dramatists discovered that the real story of, say, the Depression was not in statistics and large social changes, but in the ways it affected a family in its living room. From there it was a small step to the discoveries of the 1940s and 1950s that purely personal experiences, even those without larger social implications, were valuable and dramatic in themselves. A national literature of plays set in living rooms is a deeply democratic national literature, one that assumes that the important subjects are those that manifest themselves in the daily lives of ordinary people.

And finally "melodrama," a word with unfortunate and undeserved negative connotations. Although "melodramatic" is popularly used as a criticism of literature that invokes shallow or excessive emotional effects, the noun merely refers to a serious play with no pretension to tragedy. It is worth noting that few American dramatists aspire to high tragedy; indeed, the other characteristics already enumerated, particularly realism and the domestic setting, militate against any such ambition. Once again an essentially democratic impulse is at work, in the assumption that the important events of life, the things worth writing plays about, are the things that happen to the essentially ordinary, not the heroic. . . .

This, then, is a literary history with a plot. For various historical and artistic reasons the stylistic outline of the twentieth-century American drama has a clearly discernible arc. An art form that was essentially born afresh at the beginning of the century went through a period of exploration and experiment culminating in the discovery that one style was more amenable to American tastes and more adaptable to the demands that different writers made on it. That style—realistic contemporary middle-class domestic melodrama—was to become the dominant and artistically most fertile and flexible mode, the one in which the greatest American dramatists were able to create the greatest American plays, and in which writers with widely varying agendas could offer psychological insights, political criticism or spiritual counsel. So absolute was the superiority for American dramatic purposes of domestic realism that when, soon after the middle of the century, some significant changes in the theatrical structure led to another period of experiment and exploration, the centre held. Artistic discoveries were made—some of them greatly enriching the dramatic vocabulary—but domestic realism retained its place as the native and natural American dramatic style as new generations of dramatists continued to discover its flexibility and power. . . .

DOMESTIC REALISM IN THE 1950s

In one important way the drama of the 1950s turned away from the direction set in the 1930s. Although some playwrights, notably Arthur Miller, continued to address social and political issues by dramatizing their effect on the everyday domestic lives of ordinary people, others, led by Tennessee Williams (and anticipated by O'Neill), returned to the focus on psychological exploration that had been the concern of the realistic dramatists of the 1920s. Now, however, the concentration was not so much on explaining abnormal behaviour through Freudian analysis, as George Kelly, for example, had done in *Craig's Wife*, but on expressing and illuminating the emotions that lay beneath both normal and abnormal behaviour. Not the least of Method acting's contributions to the theatre was its making playwrights and audiences as well as actors aware of "subtext," the emotional drama going on beneath the most mundane of conversations. For some of the best American dramatists of the 1950s and thereafter, the subject to be dramatized was their characters' spiritual and psychic adventure, what it felt like to be alive and trying to cope in the middle of the twentieth century.

More often than not, what they discovered was that it felt rather frightening, that even their most successfully functioning characters were actually being driven by feelings of inadequacy or inability to cope with the ordinary pains and pressures of life. Plays that dramatized this insight could give the audience a sort of comfort, in the demonstration that such insecurities were not individual failings but part of the human condition. Plays that showed realistically uncertain characters coping with or triumphing over their fears provided encouragement and inspiration. So the function and capacity of domestic realism was expanded once again, to include a spiritual content and purpose, in plays that not only explained or argued, but actually offered counsel, consolation and reassurance.

Just as the American drama of the 1920s was dominated by the figure of Eugene O'Neill and the drama of the 1930s given shape and focus in the plays of Clifford Odets, the mid-century drama can be defined by the work of, in this case, two dominant figures. (As always, Eugene O'Neill, though towering over the others, stood apart from them, with little effect on his contemporaries.) There is a difference, however, and it is not just a matter of number. O'Neill was without question the best and most ambitious American dramatist of the 1920s, but he was not a part of whatever mainstream there was. Odets helped to discover and shape the mainstream dramatic mode of his decade and after, but that is clearer in hindsight than it was at the time, when he seemed to be just one talented writer among many. The

1945–60 period was clearly dominated by its two leading dramatists; virtually every serious American play of the time functioned within artistic boundaries defined by the plays of Tennessee Williams and Arthur Miller. . . .

THE INFLUENCE OF MILLER AND WILLIAMS

Williams and Miller had strikingly parallel careers. In each case some early writing led to an inauspicious New York debut: Miller's first Broadway play lasted four performances while Williams's closed out of town. Each followed with a second play that declared him to be a writer of importance, and with a third that would prove to be the finest play of his career. They went on to write some of the best American plays of the 1950s, and both ended their periods of greatest accomplishment in the early 1960s.

Beyond the parallels and the excellence of the individual plays, Williams and Miller had clearly developed dramatic styles and concerns that between them delimited both the manner and the matter of mid-century American drama. Following the lead of the previous decades, both wrote predominantly in the mode of contemporary, realistic domestic melodrama. But both helped to stretch that style a little through the introduction of symbolic or expressionistic elements that did not break or weaken the overall sense of realism. Miller followed in the direction begun by Herne[1] and Crothers[2] at the start of the century and refined by Odets and the other realists of the 1930s, by using domestic stories to reflect larger political or moral issues. Williams, perhaps moved by an impulse parallel to those that led Maxwell Anderson and Thornton Wilder to other styles, helped to move domestic realism beyond this political focus towards its new function of illuminating psychological and emotional forces within his characters. Miller repeatedly took as his subject the ordinary person placed under extraordinary pressure by his society and either destroyed by it or triumphant over it; Williams wrote of extraordinary people, frequently the freaks and misfits of humanity, trying to survive the ordinary pressures of life emotionally and spiritually. Thus Miller's plays were, in effect, vertical in their thrust, celebrating the potential for stature and greatness in the Common Man (Miller's phrase), while Williams's were horizon-

1. American dramatist James   2. American dramatist Rachel

tal, speaking of the common humanity shared by the normal and abnormal. And while Miller, in keeping with his social agenda, strove for a style of clarity and direct statement, Williams brought the instincts of a poet to the drama, speaking and allowing his characters to speak in the language of symbols, emotionalism and rhetorical flourishes.

Miller and Williams were thus not merely the outstanding American dramatists of the period. Almost all their contemporaries also wrote predominantly in the mode of domestic realism, and chose as their subjects either the social/political or the psychological/spiritual. It would be tempting, therefore, to label each of them as being of "the school of Miller" or "the school of Williams" were the concept of such "schools" simply not native to the American drama. While there are isolated cases of direct influence (Odets on Miller, Williams on Albee), what happened in the 1950s was as unplanned as what had happened in previous decades: individual writers followed their own muses, and their cumulative experience, along with audience response, gave a shape to the drama of the period. In this case, the styles and concerns of Arthur Miller and Tennessee Williams mark the ends of a very short continuum on which virtually every other serious American play of the 1950s can be placed, and thus define their age in a way that O'Neill and Odets did not define theirs.

Understanding Miller's Heroes

Gerald Weales

Gerald Weales contends that the heroes in Miller's plays are engaged in a struggle to find and maintain their identity. Their conflict, according to Weales, is in either accepting or rejecting a standard image imposed on them through society's values and prejudices. Joe Keller in *All My Sons* must kill himself to destroy the image that he has accepted from society. In *Death of a Salesman*, Willy Loman confuses society's labels with reality so a great gap exists between the actual Willy and Willy as image. John Proctor in *The Crucible* loses his identity to the hysteria of society, but, when his wife finally forgives him, he regains it.

Gerald Weales has taught graduate and undergraduate drama classes at the University of Pennsylvania, Philadelphia. His articles on drama have appeared in *Drama Survey, Tulane Drama Review*, and *Antioch Review*. Weales is also the author of *Religion in Modern English Drama*.

Arthur Miller is one of those playwrights, like Thornton Wilder, whose reputation rests on a handful of plays. The quality of that reputation changes from year to year, from critic to critic, but... after the production of his most recent play (the revision of *A View from the Bridge*), it is generally conceded, even by those who persist in not admiring his work, that Miller is one of the two playwrights of the postwar American theater who deserve any consideration as major dramatists....

There are many ways of approaching Miller's work. In the late forties, after *All My Sons* and *Death of a Salesman*, popular reviewers tended to embrace him enthusiastically, while consciously intellectual critics, displaying the careful-

From *American Drama Since World War II* by Gerald Weales (New York: Harcourt, Brace & World, 1962). Copyright ©1962 by Gerald Weales. Reprinted with permission from the author.

ness of their kind, hoped that in explaining him they might explain him away. For a time, his plays were lost in discussions of the author's politics, past and present, or were buried beneath the pointless academic quibble about whether or not they are true tragedies. Miller's own defensiveness on these two points helped feed the controversy. In the last few years, however, with no new Miller play to stir up opinion, his work has begun to be considered outside the immediate context that produced it. . . .

To me . . . the most profitable way of looking at his work is through his heroes and through the concern of each, however inarticulate, with his identity—his *name*, as both John Proctor and Eddie Carbone call it. . . .

Each of his heroes is involved, in one way or another, in a struggle that results from his acceptance or rejection of an image that is the product of his society's values and prejudices, whether that society is as small as Eddie Carbone's neighborhood or as wide as the contemporary America that helped form Willy Loman. Miller's work has followed such a pattern from the beginning. Even Ben, the hero of *They Too Arise*, a now happily forgotten prize winner from the mid-thirties, has to decide whether he is to be the man that his middle-class, small-businessman father expects or the comrade that his radical brother demands; the play ends, of course, in leftist affirmation, but the conflict has been in terms of opposed images, both of which are assumed to have validity for Ben. The hero of *The Man Who Had All the Luck* (1944), Miller's first produced play, accepts the town's view of him as a man who has succeeded through luck not ability; he assumes that all luck must turn and, in his obsession, almost brings disaster on his head until his wife convinces him that he should reject the town's rationalizing bromide and accept the principle that man makes his own luck. In his novel *Focus* (1945), a fantasy-tract, his anti-Semitic hero finally accepts the label that his neighbors force on him; he admits that he is a Jew. Most of Miller's short stories reflect the same kind of preoccupation with the self that someone else expects the hero to be; in one of his most recent stories, "I Don't Need You Any More" (*Esquire*, December 1959), the five-year-old hero's idea of himself is formed on half-understood perceptions picked up from his parents and the adult world they live in, the only society that he recognizes outside himself. The lament and the longing implicit in Martin's thought—"If only he *looked* like his father and his brother!"—is a small echo of the bewilderment that haunts all the Miller heroes who do the right things and come to the wrong ends.

JOE KELLER VS. SOCIETY IN *ALL MY SONS*

In *All My Sons* (1947), Miller's first successful play, Joe Keller, who is admittedly a good husband and a good father, fails to be the good man, the good citizen that his son Chris demands. "I'm his father and he's my son, and if there's something bigger than that I'll put a bullet in my head!" Chris makes clear that, for him, there is something bigger than the family, and Joe commits suicide. Much more interesting than the unmasking and punishment of Joe's crime (he shipped out cracked cylinder heads during the war and let his partner take the blame and go to jail) is Joe as a peculiarly American product. He is a self-made man, a successful businessman "with the imprint of the machine-shop worker and boss still upon him." There is nothing ruthless about Joe, no hint of the robber baron in his make-up; his ambitions are small—a comfortable home for his family, a successful business to pass on to his sons—but he is not completely fastidious in achieving his goals. Not only has he accepted the American myth of the primacy of the family, his final excuse for all his actions, but he has adopted as a working instrument the familiar attitude that there is a difference between morality and business ethics. Not that he could ever phrase it that way. "I'm in business, a man is in business . . ." he begins his explanation, his plea for understanding, and moves on to that dimly lit area where the other man's culpability is his forgiveness.

When Miller at last moves in on Joe, brings Chris and discovery to destroy him, there is no longer any possibility of choice. His fault, according to Miller and Chris, is that he does not recognize any allegiance to society at large; his world, as he mistakenly says of that of his dead son Larry, "had a forty-foot front, it ended at the building line." Joe's shortness of vision, however, is a product of his society. Even Chris shares his goals: "If I have to grub for money all day long at least at evening I want it beautiful. I want a family, I want some kids, I want to build something I can give myself to." The neighbors, in the figure of Sue, respect Joe's methods: "They give him credit for being smart." At the end of the play, finally confronted with another alternative ("But I think to him they were all my sons"), Joe Keller, in killing himself, destroys the image that he has accepted.

WILLY LOMAN VS. SOCIETY IN *DEATH OF A SALESMAN*

There is a disturbing patness about *All My Sons*, an exemplary working out of the conflict that is as didactic as Chris's more extended speeches. With *Death of a Salesman* (1949), Miller escapes into richness. The ambiguity that occasionally touches the characters in the earlier play, that makes the supposedly admirable idealist son sound at times like a hanging judge, suffuses the playwright's second success, his finest play. It might be possible to reduce the play to some kind of formula, to suggest that Biff's end-of-the-play declaration, "I know who I am, kid," is a positive statement, a finger pointing in some verifiable direction, a refutation of all the beliefs to which Willy clings and for which he dies. Miller suggests, in his Introduction to the *Collected Plays*, that Biff does embody an "opposing system" to the "law of success" which presumably kills Willy, but there are almost as many contradictions in Miller's Introduction as there are in his play. Since the last scene, the Requiem, is full of irony— Charley's romantic eulogy of the Salesman, Linda's failure to understand ("I made the last payment on the house today. . . . We're free and clear"), Happy's determination to follow in his father's failed footsteps—there is no reason to assume that some of the irony does not rub off on Biff. We have been with the lying Lomans so long, have seen them hedge their bets and hide their losses in scene after self-deluding scene, that it is at least forgivable if we respect Willy's integrity as a character (if not as a man) and suspect that Biff is still his son. The play after all, ends with the funeral; there is no sequel.

When we meet Willy Loman, he, like Joe Keller, is past the point of choice, but his play tells us that there are at least three will-of-the-wisp ideals—father figures, all—that Willy might have chosen to follow. The first is his own father, the inventor, the flute maker, the worker-with-his-hands, who walked away one day and left the family to shift for itself. His is the flute melody that opens the play, "small and fine, telling of grass and trees and the horizon." From what we hear of him, he was a man who did not make his fortune because he did not know that a fortune was a thing worth making and, if his desertion of his family means anything, he needed the world's good opinion as little as he needed its idea of conventional success. The chances of Willy's going the way of his father are as dead as the frontier, of course; so when the flute appears in the play it is no more than a suggestion of a very vague might-have-been. Nor is the second possible choice, that embodied in the figure of Ben, a likely one for Willy; it is difficult to imagine him among the business buccaneers. For that reason, perhaps, Miller has chosen to make a comic caricature of Ben: "Why, boys, when I was seventeen I walked into the jungle, and when I was twenty-one I walked out. And by God I was rich." Ben, with his assurance, his ruthlessness ("Never fight fair with a stranger, boy"), his connections in Africa and Alaska, looms a little larger than life in Willy's mind, half cartoon, half romance. There is romance enough—liberally laced with sentiment—in the ideal that Willy does choose, Dave Singleman, the old salesman who, at eighty-four, could, through the strength of his personality, sit in a hotel room and command buyers. Willy admires Singleman for dying "the death of a salesman, in his green velvet slippers in the smoker of the New York, New Haven and Hartford," without ever recognizing that there is more than one way to kill a salesman.

A PLEA FOR WILLY

Willy Loman in Death of a Salesman *is an intense and well-meaning man who is troubled and bewildered by the messages that society is giving him. His limitations, his misguided choices, and his confusion in life make him a thoroughly human character. In this excerpt from the play, Willy's wife, Linda, conveys her sympathy and understanding for her husband's predicament to her sons.*

I don't say he's a great man. Willy Loman never made a lot of money. His name was never in the paper. He's not the finest character that ever lived. But he's a human being, and a terrible thing is happening to him. So attention must be paid. He's not to be allowed to fall into his grave like an old dog. Attention, attention must be finally paid to such a person.

Willy can no more be Dave Singleman than he can be his father or his brother Ben. From the conflicting success images that wander through his troubled brain comes Willy's double ambition—to be rich and to be loved. As he tells Ben, "the wonder of this country [is] that a man can end with diamonds here on the basis of being liked!" From Andrew

Carnegie, then, to Dale Carnegie. Willy's faith in the magic of "personal attractiveness" as a way to success carries him beyond cause and effect to necessity; he assumes that success falls inevitably to the man with the right smile, the best line, the most charm, the man who is not only liked, but well liked. He has completely embraced the American myth, born of the advertisers, that promises us love and a fortune as soon as we clear up our pimples, stop underarm perspiration, learn to play the piano; for this reason, the brand names that turn up in Willy's speeches are more than narrow realism. He regularly confuses labels with reality. . . .

The distance between the actual Willy and Willy as image is so great when the play opens that he can no longer lie to himself with conviction; what the play gives us is the final disintegration of a man who has never even approached his idea of what by rights he ought to have been. His ideal may have been the old salesman in his green velvet slippers, but his model is that mythic figure, the traveling salesman of the dirty joke. Willy tries to be a kidder, a caution, a laugh-a-minute; he shares his culture's conviction that personality is a matter of mannerism and in the sharing develops a style that is compounded of falseness, the mock assurance of what Happy calls "the old humor, the old confidence." His act, however, is as much for himself as it is for his customers. The play shows quite clearly that from the beginning of his career Willy has lied about the size of his sales, the warmth of his reception, the number of his friends. It is true that he occasionally doubts himself, assumes that he is too noisy and undignified, that he is not handsome enough ("I'm fat. I'm very—foolish to look at"), but usually he rationalizes his failure. His continuing self-delusion and his occasional self-awareness serve the same purpose; they keep him from questioning the assumptions that lie beneath his failure and his pretense of success. By the time we get to him, his struggle to hold onto his dream (if not for himself, then for his sons) has become so intense that all control is gone; past and present are one to him, and so are fact and fiction. . . .

JOHN PROCTOR VS. SOCIETY IN *THE CRUCIBLE*

Joe Keller and Willy Loman find ready-made societal images to attach themselves to and both become victims of the attachment. Society is not nearly so passive in Miller's next play, *The Crucible* (1953). Salem tries to force John Proctor to accept a particular image of himself, but he chooses to die. Although there are occasional voices in the earlier plays (the neighbors in *All My Sons*, the bartender in *Death of a Salesman*) who speak for society, Miller operates for the most part on the assumption that his audience knows and shares the ideas that work on the Kellers and the Lomans. He cannot be that certain in *The Crucible*. Whether we are to accept his Salem as historical or as an analogy for the United States in the early fifties, Miller needs to create a mood of mass hysteria in which guilt and confession become public virtues. For this reason, Proctor is not so intensively on stage as the protagonists of the earlier plays are; the playwright has to work up a setting for him, has to give his attention to the accusers, the court, the town. . . .

Although Proctor is never completely successful as a character, Miller makes a real effort to convince us that he is more than the blunt, not so bright good man he appears to be; and once again Miller works in terms of societal concepts. The Proctor who appears in the novelistic notes that Miller has sprinkled through the text of the published play is not quite the Proctor of the play itself; but there are similarities. We are to assume that Proctor is a solid man, but an independent one, not a man to fit lightly into anyone else's mold. When we meet him, however, he is suffering under a burden of guilt—intensified by his belief that Elizabeth is continually judging him. Miller makes it clear that in sleeping with Abigail Williams, Proctor has become "a sinner not only against the moral fashion of the time, but against his own vision of decent conduct." In Act III, when he admits in open court that he is a lecher, he says, "A man will not cast away his good name." When he is finally faced with the choice of death or confession (that he consorted with the devil), his guilt as an adulterer becomes confused with his innocence as a witch; one sin against society comes to look like another, or so he rationalizes. In the last act, however, Elizabeth in effect absolves him of the sin of adultery, gives him back the name he lost in court, and clears the way for him to reject the false confession and to give his life: "How may I live without my name?"

Eddie Carbone vs. Society in *A View from the Bridge*

Eddie Carbone in *A View from the Bridge* (1955; revised, 1956) also dies crying out for his name, but when he asks

Marco to "gimme my name" he is asking for a lie that will let him live and, failing that, for death. Eddie is unusual among the Miller heroes in that he accepts the rules and prejudices of his society, an Italian neighborhood in Brooklyn, and dies because he violates them. Early in the play, Eddie warns Catherine to be closemouthed about the illegal immigrants (the "submarines") who are coming to live with them; he tells her with approbation about the brutal punishment meted out to an informer. By the end of the play, the "passion that had moved into his body, like a stranger," as Alfieri calls it, so possesses Eddie that to rid himself of the presence of Rodolpho he is willing to commit an act that he abhors as much as his society does. Miller's own comments on the play and the lines that he gives to Alfieri, a cross between the Greek chorus and Mary Worth,[1] indicate that he sees Eddie in the grip of a force that is almost impersonal in its inevitability, its terribleness, "the awesomeness of a passion which . . . despite even its destruction of the moral beliefs of the individual, proceeds to magnify its power over him until it destroys him." The action in *View* seems to me somewhat more complicated than the clean line Miller suggests; its hero is more than a leaf blown along on winds out of ancient Calabria.[2] Eddie chooses to become an informer; his choice is so hedged with rationalization—his convincing himself that Rodolpho is homosexual, that he is marrying Catherine for citizenship papers—that he is never conscious of his motivation. He comes closer and closer to putting a label on his incestuous love for Catherine (although technically she is his niece, functionally she is his daughter) and his homosexual attraction to Rodolpho (how pathetically he goes round and round to keep from saying *queer*). By comparison, informing is a simpler breach of code, one that has justification in the world outside the neighborhood. It is almost as though he takes on the name *informer* to keep from wearing some name that is still more terrible to him, only to discover that he cannot live under the lesser label either.

THE HERO TRAPPED BY SOCIETY

"It is not enough any more to know that one is at the mercy of social pressures," Miller writes in "On Social Plays"; "it is necessary to understand that such a sealed fate cannot be

1. comic strip heroine   2. a district of southern Italy

accepted." Each of his four heroes is caught in a trap compounded of social and psychological forces and each one is destroyed. Miller is concerned that their deaths not be dismissed as insignificant, the crushing of little men by big forces. His description of Eddie Carbone expresses his opinion of all his heroes: "he possesses or exemplifies the wondrous and humane fact that he too can be driven to what in the last analysis is a sacrifice of himself for his conception, however misguided, of right, dignity, and justice.". . .

The theme that recurs in all of his plays—the relationship between a man's identity and the image that society demands of him—is a major one; in one way or another it has been the concern of most serious playwrights. A big theme is not enough, of course; Miller has the ability to invest it with emotion. He is sometimes sentimental, sometimes romantic about both his characters and their situations; but sentiment and romance, if they can command an audience without drowning it, are not necessarily vices. Even in *A Memory of Two Mondays,* in which he peoples his stage with stereotypes, he manages, in the end, to make Bert's departure touching. The test of the good commercial playwright is the immediate reaction of an audience; the test of the good playwright is how well his plays hold up under continuing observation. Each time I go back to *All My Sons,* to *The Crucible,* to *A View from the Bridge,* the faults become more ominous, but in each of these plays there are still scenes that work as effectively as they did when I first saw the play. *Death of a Salesman* is something else again. It does not merely hold its own, it grows with each rereading. Those people who go in for good-better-best labels—I am not one of them—would be wise, when they draw up their list of American plays, to put *Death of a Salesman* very near the top.

The Individual and Society in Miller's Plays

William B. Dillingham

William B. Dillingham states that a major theme in Miller's plays is the struggle of the individual to find a place in society where he is securely loved and in turn feels a sense of responsibility for others. Dillingham argues that tragedy occurs when a character either fails to recognize his place or forfeits his place for false values. Disconnected from society, the confused individual finds it difficult to maintain a sense of integrity and conscience. Dillingham assesses the relationship of the individual in society in four of Miller's protagonists: Joe Keller in *All My Sons*, Willy Loman in *Death of a Salesman*, John Proctor in *The Crucible*, and Eddie Carbone in *A View from the Bridge*.

William Dillingham is a professor of English at Emory University, Atlanta, Georgia. He is the author of *Frank Norris: The Fiction of Force.*

Man's obligation to assume his rightful place in a world unified by love and a sense of responsibility is the central thesis of Arthur Miller's critical essays and the major theme of his plays. Tragedy occurs when a man fails to recognize his place in society or when he gives it up because of false values. Miller's goal as a serious playwright, he feels, is to point man toward "a world in which the human being can live as a naturally political, naturally private, naturally engaged person." Such a world was the Greek *polis*, where the people, Miller says, "were *engaged,* they could not imagine the good life excepting as it brought each person into close contact with civic matters.... The preoccupation of the Greek drama with ultimate law, with the Grand Design, so to speak, was therefore an expression of a basic assumption of the people, who could not yet conceive, luckily, that any man could

From "Arthur Miller and the Loss of Conscience" by William B. Dillingham, *Emory University Quarterly*, vol. 16, Spring 1960, pp. 40-50. Reprinted with permission of the author.

longer prosper unless his polis prospered. The individual was at one with his society; his conflicts with it were, in our terms, like family conflicts the opposing sides of which nevertheless shared mutuality of feeling and responsibility."

Miller's tragedies are about men who are not "at one" with society because they have sinned against it or have refused to assume their rightful place in it. Unfortunately, such men are representative products of the complex modern world, where man finds it difficult if not impossible to identify himself with society "except in the form of a truce with it." "The best we have been able to do," Miller writes, "is speak of a 'duty' to society, and this implies sacrifice or self-deprivation. To think of an individual fulfilling his subjective needs through social action . . . is difficult for us to imagine." Yet man can retain his integrity of "conscience" only if he is a part of the world of "feeling and responsibility" for others. For Miller, the loss of conscience is evidenced by a terrible unconsciousness, an unawareness of fundamental values and of what constitutes human dignity. The pity and fear traditionally associated with the kathartic value of tragedy can best be experienced, Miller feels, by observing those who have lost conscience and have thereby been isolated from the "Grand Design." Central in the four tragedies, *All My Sons, Death of a Salesman, The Crucible,* and *A View from the Bridge,* is the loss of conscience (and the efforts to regain it).

JOE KELLER'S SPLIT FROM SOCIETY

Joe Keller of *All My Sons* has committed a grave antisocial act in allowing faulty and dangerous airplane engines to be sent from his wartime factory for use in combat. Keller represents, Miller has stated, "a threat to society," and his crime "is seen as having roots in a certain relationship of the individual to society, and to a certain indoctrination he embodies, which, if dominant, can mean a jungle existence for all of us no matter how high our buildings soar. And it is in this sense that loneliness is socially meaningful in these plays." Yet Joe Keller is not villainous. He does not exhibit in his personal life any of the brutality and cruelty generally associated with villains; indeed, he is a loving, dutiful husband and father. But it is precisely this virtuous love for his family that sows the seeds of tragedy. "Joe Keller's trouble," Miller writes, "is not that he cannot tell right from wrong but that his cast of mind cannot admit that he, personally, has any viable connection with his world, his universe, or his society. He is not a partner in society, but an incorporated member, so to speak, and you cannot sue personally the officers of a corporation.". . .

WILLY LOMAN'S SPLIT FROM SOCIETY

Like Joe Keller, Willy Loman is characterized by his fanatic allegiance to a dream at the expense of conscience. In defending *Death of a Salesman* against the charge of being anti-capitalistic, Miller has written: "The most decent man in *Death of a Salesman* is a capitalist whose aims are not different from Willy Loman's. The great difference between them is that Charley is not a fanatic." Willy insists upon trying to believe that he is a successful, "well-liked" salesman. Yet this is not a conception which he can really fulfill, as only Biff seems to admit. "They've laughed at Dad for years," Biff says, "and you know why? Because we don't belong in this nuthouse of a city! We should be mixing cement on some open plain, or—or carpenters. A carpenter is allowed to whistle!" Willy's false dream of his position in life is an expensive one. For he becomes, as Miller puts it, "a man superbly alone with his sense of not having touched . . . the image of private man in a world full of strangers, a world that is not home nor even an open battle ground but only galaxies of high promise over a fear of falling." In short, *Death of a Salesman* is the portrait of a man who has given up conscience, that which is most fundamentally himself, for a place in society that can never be his. There was "more of him in that front stoop" he made with his hands, Biff says, "than in all the sales he ever made."

In losing his identity in an illusion of success and security, Willy Loman is strongly influenced by the same idea that dominated the F. Scott Fitzgerald's Gatsbys and the Sinclair Lewis's Babbitts. Reared on the American success story, he watched his brother Ben go into the jungle poor and come out rich. Ben constantly exemplifies for Willy the glory of going from rags to riches. At times Willy actually questions the values he is stressing to his sons and admits that he feels "temporary" about himself. In this state of mind he seeks advice of Ben: "Ben, how should I teach them?" Ben's answer is the "American dream" in summary: "William, when I walked into the jungle, I was seventeen. When I walked out I was twenty-one. And, by God, I was rich!" Reassured, Willy feels that Ben has reached the end of the rainbow, and he is ready to follow him: "That's just the spirit I want to imbue them with! To walk into a jungle! I was right! I was right! I was right!"

A DEFINITION OF SOCIAL DRAMA

Arthur Miller writes social drama, a genre that, according to John Gassner and Morris Sweetkind in their anthology Introducing the Drama, *examines individuals in society and focuses on their problems and conflicts.*

Three more or less distinct types of serious drama have appeared frequently in the theatre of the Western world. *Tragedy* takes life seriously by dealing with meaningful suffering and showing men and women struggling with their fate. *Social drama* examines life in society and focuses attention on its problems and conflicts. *Melodrama*, in concentrating on crimes and catastrophes that keep the playgoer in suspense or fill him with excitement, highlights—often quite sensationally—the world of good and evil with which men are concerned in reality and in fantasy. . . .

To some degree "social drama" is likely to be encountered almost everywhere in the modern theatre because of our great interest in political conflict, social ideas, and the influence of environment. Man is a social animal, and naturally interested in the stability and welfare of his society. He is also apt to be concerned with problems of social behavior and government that require active participation on his part and that make him choose one side or another in a controversy or a political conflict. In the modern theatre, which reflects the modern world, playwrights have often dealt directly with social and economic problems. They have done so "topically," presenting a specific "topic" of immediate interest and urgency as in plays about presidential elections such as *State of the Union* by Howard Lindsay and Russel Crouse, and in *The Best Man* by Gore Vidal; or they have written about society in terms that are neither topical nor local in essence but "universal." Such a play is *An Enemy of the People*, written in 1882 by Henrik Ibsen. Its subject is the conflict between the individual and his community when his conscience clashes with the materialistic interests of his fellow citizens. The term *social drama* is used most appropriately when a play gives unmistakable priority to the social or political conflict, and our attention is not diverted from it by other considerations.

Willy encounters another aspect of the American dream in his wife Linda, for whom security is the most important goal in life. Paradoxically, Linda genuinely loves and respects her husband, but she is a contributing cause in his tragedy. From the first she believes in Willy as the "well-liked" supersalesman. When he complains of his small number of sales, her confidence in him is unshaken: "Well, next week you'll do better," she tells him. At times Willy seems on the verge of recognizing his mediocrity as a salesman, but Linda resupplies him with the stuff his dreams are made on. "I don't know the reason for it," Willy tells Linda, "but they just pass me by. I'm not noticed." In answer Linda offers more encouragement than understanding: "But you're doing wonderful, dear." And when Willy has a chance to give up selling to go to Alaska, she convinces him that he should not go, that security is everything.

Probably Willy Loman would have failed in Alaska as he did at home, but the important point is that Linda believed in the illusion of her husband as the successful salesman perhaps more than Willy himself did. And instead of encouraging him to be himself—to be a carpenter or a plumber or a bricklayer—and to identify himself with real and fundamental values, she urges him to remain as he is, "alone, without the sense of having touched," in the name of security. Linda's emphasis on material security and her failure in understanding are reflected in her final speech at Willy's graveside: "Forgive me, dear. I can't cry. I don't know what it is, but I can't cry. I don't understand it. Why did you ever do that? . . . Why did you do it? I search and search and I search, and I can't understand it, Willy. I made the last payment on the house today. Today, dear. And there'll be nobody home. We're free and clear.". . .

But *Death of a Salesman*, as Miller has pointed out, is not meant to be a pessimistic play. If it focuses on Willy Loman's loss of conscience, it is also the story of Biff Loman and his struggle to regain his identity. Biff's values were distorted by his father, who felt it unimportant that his son was a thief as long as the boy was well-liked. Biff suddenly changes, however, when he discovers the woman in Willy's hotel room. He then sees Willy Loman as he has never seen him before, false to others and to himself. And through his determination not to follow Willy's example, not to go through life pretending, Biff is able to find himself. At his father's grave he tells Happy, "I know who I am." He has gained what Willy never found, his rightful position in society.

As in *All My Sons*, so again in *The Crucible*, Arthur Miller has emphasized the necessity for man's fidelity to others as well as to himself by stressing the horror of the antisocial act. In *The Crucible* Miller has dramatized the Salem witch hunt, one of the most terrible examples of how man may sin against his fellow beings. In his remarks on the play Miller has made it quite clear that he meant to compare the witch hunt with the McCarthy investigations. During this time of "McCarthyism," Miller has written, "conscience was no longer a private matter but one of state administration." He continues: "I saw men handing conscience to other men and thanking other men for the opportunity of doing so. I wished for a way to write a play that would be sharp, that would lift out of the morass of subjectivism the squirming, singled, defined process which would show that the sin of public terror is that it divests man of conscience, of himself. It was a theme not unrelated to those that invested the previous plays."

JOHN PROCTOR'S ACT OF CONSCIENCE

Although the theme is the same, the tragic hero of *The Crucible* is different from the heroes of the other plays. John Proctor, unlike Joe Keller, refuses to commit the antisocial action. That is, he loses his life because he will not admit that he is a witch, a confession that would save his own life but make the others who would not confess seem guilty and thereby justify the trials. He refuses to sign the confession because it would mean handing his conscience to the judges, as he puts it, a loss of his "name." When Danforth asks why he will not sign, Proctor replies: "Because it is my name! Because I cannot have another in my life! Because I lie and sign myself to lies! Because I am not worth the dust on the feet of them that hang! How may I live without my name?" John Proctor is not an especially good or brave person. Indeed, he has previously committed adultery with the chief accuser of the witches, Abigail Williams, and this relationship is one of the main causes of the witch hunt. Abigail desires Proctor's wife to hang so that she may have him. Proctor has felt his guilt strongly, and, as Miller tells us, "has come to regard himself as a kind of fraud." His adultery and guilt have prevented him from feeling at one with his community. From his wife, too, he has been spiritually and mentally separated since his sin. But Proctor, like Biff Loman, finds himself during the course of the play. He openly admits to the community that he is a "lecher" in order to save his wife, and after again feeling himself a part of the same brotherhood with the noble Rebecca Nurse and Giles Cory, the two "witches" who refuse to sign a false confession, he will not lose what he has gained. The central crucible, or trial, of *The Crucible* is John Proctor's personal test. He has a choice between life without conscience or death. He chooses to save his identity, his "name," even though it means his death. . . .

EDDIE CARBONE'S SPLIT FROM SOCIETY

In *A View from the Bridge* the plot again focuses on an antisocial action, Eddie Carbone's betrayal of the immigrants. The longshoreman, Eddie Carbone, has taken his wife's niece into his home and supplied her needs as if she were his own child. As Catherine approaches young womanhood, however, his love for her becomes more than that of father for daughter. The coming of the immigrants Rodolpho and Marco stimulates his passion for Catherine. And when Rodolpho and Catherine indicate their desire to be married, Eddie must make a choice: he may simply acquiesce in the marriage of Catherine and thus fight against the intense passion he has for her, or he may keep Catherine in his household but only by betraying Rodolpho and Marco, who are guilty of illegal entry, to the authorities. After going to Mr. Alfieri, the lawyer, to inquire if the law will aid him in stopping Catherine's marriage to Rodolpho, Eddie succumbs to his passion and causes not only Rodolpho and Marco to be arrested but also two other immigrants whom he does not even know.

In betraying Rodolpho and Marco, Eddie violates a code of behavior with which he has previously identified himself. Early in the play Eddie indicates his accordance with the idea of helping immigrants in order that they may get a start. "It's an honor, B." he tells his wife. "I mean it. I was just thinkin' before, comin' home, suppose my father didn't come to this country, and I was starvin' like them over there . . . and I had people in America could help me a couple of months? The man would be honored to lend me a place to sleep." Commenting on Eddie's loss of conscience, Miller has written: "The maturing of Eddie's need to destroy Rodolpho was consequently seen in the context which could make it of real moment, for the betrayal achieves its true proportions as it flies in the face of the mores administered by Eddie's conscience—which is also the conscience of his friends, co-workers, and neighbors and not just his own autonomous creation." Eddie's action thus not only prevents the immigrants from feeding their starving families in Italy but also isolates him from his society, which recognizes the need of man to help his brothers. Eddie's need to reidentify himself with his society is suggested by his asking Marco to give him back his "name." "I want my name, Marco," Eddie says. "Now gimme my name." To Eddie Carbone as well as to John Proctor, name symbolizes a connection, a communion, with one's fellow beings without which we become hollow.

The settings and the social order in Arthur Miller's tragedies are modern. Even in *The Crucible*, where Miller goes to history for his plot and setting, there is an intended parallel to a modern situation. His primary interest, however, is traditional, for he is chiefly concerned with the individual and with the problem of moral decision. If his characters live in the modern world depicted by determinists like novelists Theodore Dreiser and John Galsworthy, they, like the heroes of Shakespeare and Hawthorne, must make their own choices. Tragedy occurs when they lose conscience, when they choose to ignore their responsible place in society. For this age Miller represents an unusual synthesis: the artist who is profoundly concerned with both the *polis* and the integrity and responsibility of the individual.

The Role of the Family in Miller's Plays

William J. Newman

Much of the conflict and tension of Arthur Miller's plays is played out in small scale in the relationships and interactions among family members. According to William J. Newman, if Miller's characters are to find affection and certainty anywhere, they must look to the family. Business, the other basic social unit, cannot play the same role because it is insecure, impersonal, and cutthroat. However, Newman suggests, the absence of continuity in American life is the element that condemns the family to failure. It is this failure of the American family that Miller describes in his work.

William J. Newman taught in the Department of Government at Boston University. He contributes to many magazines and is the author of *Liberalism and the Retreat from Politics*.

Although there is no fundamental 'philosophical' view which can be derived from Miller's plays, there is nevertheless a persistent and continuing problem which gives him the raw material of his plays and the means of expressing his ideas. It is a problem which enables Miller to narrow down the situation of universal man to the concrete situation of a particular American man. The relationship of the American father and son and of both to the American family in the American 'situation' provides him, not with his themes, but with the raw material of tensions and conflicts between human beings. (Note how uninteresting and undeveloped the women are in Miller's plays; they witness the drama but have little to contribute to it.) For Arthur Miller it is not just the salesman which is interesting and which he is discussing, but the salesman as a family man; Willy Loman's

From "Book Reviews: The Plays of Arthur Miller" by William J. Newman, *Twentieth Century*, vol. 164, no. 981, November 1958, pp. 491-96. Reprinted by permission of the author.

greatest and most immediate failure was not his failure to sell whatever it was he was selling, but as a man in relationship to his son, a failure of love. His significance comes from the *fact* of the American family . . . and its failure. Miller evidently has some need for such a factual basis for his drama for he records in his introduction how his earlier (unpublished) plays were diffuse for lack of 'cause and effect, hard actions, facts, the geometry of relationships.'

THE ROLE OF THE AMERICAN FAMILY

What kind of 'hard actions, facts' does the family in America provide for Arthur Miller? The American family, it should be understood, is excellent material not only for a humorist but for someone who takes life seriously, for it is a constantly fragile, constantly disintegrating attempt to create a personal framework of affection and loyalty in a world where class, institutional and local loyalties have been reduced to a minimum or do not exist at all. Critic Richard Hoggart has claimed that W.H. Auden left Britain for America because British life was too cozy. Whatever American life is, it is not cozy; there are none of the institutional—and family—protections which give the British middle class at least a semblance of security, of 'place' in a society. The American family not only serves the usual functions of a family, but more than elsewhere becomes a last-ditch stand to erect a *place* of affection and certainty, of refuge from the wider and brutal world of impersonality. The existentialist attempt to *found* oneself takes many forms, but for the American middle-class man it is above all else the family. The other important social group in America, the business unit, is by nature insecure, for within it the individual is always in danger of falling out; he is always under ruthless pressure; business 'friends' are notoriously unable—even if willing—to help when help is needed, a Rotary club is simply a mask for cut-throat business competition, while social class is an escalator which takes one up or down depending on the play of the cards.

The poor American male, if he is not to be left desolate, must establish solidarity through and within the family; hence it is that everything must be done for the family, that all the actions of the husband in the wider world are thought of in terms of what it will do for the family; nothing must be allowed to stand in the way of maintaining the tenuous stability of the family in a world devoted to inhuman relationships, and, if the result is often to make the male the slave of the family, that is a price he chooses and pays willingly. The American businessman is not selfish; there is no one who is more of a self-made sacrifice. Yet the sacrifice is considered worth while, because only within the family in America is there a chance of affection and place in return for sacrifice.

Thus the accuracy of Keller's poignant cry in *All My Sons* when he is revealed to his son as corrupt.

> MOTHER: Joe, Joe.... It don't excuse it that you did it for the family.
> KELLER: It's got to excuse it!
> MOTHER: There's something bigger than the family to him.
> KELLER: Nothin' is bigger.... (desperately, lost). For you, Kate, for both of you, that's all I ever lived for.

THE FAILURE OF THE AMERICAN FAMILY

But this American family is founded out of thin air; it has no tradition of itself, no social support (quite the contrary, all the forces of society work against it); it is usually the creation of two persons who do know each other's past, who come from different geographical areas and social classes, who have different ideas and creeds, and whose children move to different cities and different ideas. In short, it lacks almost every element of continuity; the very conditions of American life which dictate the peculiar aim of the American family also condemn it to the failure of achieving that aim. It is this failure which Arthur Miller has described in his plays. If the American family is a desperate effort in the face of social loneliness ('loneliness is socially meaningful in these plays'), its very desperation provides the facts for an analysis of man in America and elsewhere.

The substance of Miller's plays is therefore bottomed on a particular American experience. In each of his plays (with the exception of *The Crucible*, which is explicitly political in intent) the central situation centres around a child-father relationship in which the child is at an age when it is about to break loose from the family; in each case the father is faced with the consequent breakdown of the family-world he had tried to create; in each case the conflict between the child and father takes place in terms of the wider world breaching the walls of protection the father had built around the family; in each case the father is corrupt and is revealed to be corrupt by his child; and in each case this corruption leads

THE TELEVISION FAMILY OF THE 1950s

While Arthur Miller was writing about the conflicts and tensions in the American family, television was broadcasting an antiseptic, idealized portrait of family life, claims David Halberstam, author of The Fifties. *Popular television programs of the midfifties, such as* The Adventures of Ozzie and Harriet, Father Knows Best, *and* Leave it to Beaver, *centered on middle-class families functioning peacefully in an unflawed America.*

Moms and dads never raised their voices at each other in anger. Perhaps the dads thought the moms were not good drivers, and the moms thought the dads were absentminded when it came to following instructions in the kitchen, but this was a peaceable kingdom. There were no drugs. Keeping a family car out too late at night seemed to be the height of insubordination. No family difference was so irreconcilable that it could not be cleared up and straightened out within the allotted twenty-two minutes. Moms and dads never stopped loving each other. Sibling love was always greater than sibling rivalry. No child was favored, no one was stunted. None of the dads hated what they did, though it was often unclear what they actually did. Whatever it was, it was respectable and valuable; it was white-collar and it allowed them to live in the suburbs (the networks were well aware of modern demographics) and not to worry very much about money. Money was never discussed, and the dark shadow of poverty never fell over their homes, but no one made too much or they might lose their connection with the pleasantly comfortable middle-class families who watched the show and who were considered the best consumers in the country. These television families were to be not merely a reflection of their viewers but role models for them as well. . . .

To millions of other Americans, coming from flawed homes, it often seemed hopelessly unfair to look in on families like this. Millions of kids growing up in homes filled with anger and tension often felt the failure was theirs. It was their fault that their homes were messier, their parents less human (in fact they were, of course, more human) and less understanding than the television parents in whose homes they so often longed to live. As Beaver Cleaver (a rascal, with a predilection for trouble, but harmless and engaging trouble) once told June Cleaver (who was almost always well turned out in sweater and skirts), "You know, Mom, when we're in a mess, you kind of make things seem not so messy." "Well," answered June, "isn't that sort of what mothers are for?"

the father to choose death as the penalty for destroying his own ideal. The pattern is so strictly followed—even in the curtain raiser, *A Memory of Two Mondays*, where the warehouse gang acts as the family to Bert—that it is clear that the failure of these families has given the central focus of Miller's work so far.

The meaning of that failure lies in the destruction of the family as a bulwark against social loneliness by the very values which caused its creation. Keller, in *All My Sons*, makes a corrupt profit in the war because if he did not the economic basis of the family would have disappeared, but his corruption turns his son against him and destroys the family. Willy Loman, in *The Death of a Salesman*, lives by corrupt values because that is all he knows; thus he kills the whole purpose which the family held for him, the love of Biff. And finally, Eddie, in *A View from the Bridge* represents an ultimate and a logical end of love within the family—incest. (It is significant that Eddie is a working-class figure; such a conclusion to the middle-class ideal of a family is best located elsewhere than on the middle-class hearth.) The avid, single-minded pursuit of love within the family causes the corruption which destroys the family. What is implicit in all the other plays becomes manifest through Eddie's brutal sense of logic; the family itself is threatened by the love which created it. Yet, what else is possible in America? What other possibility was there for Keller, Willy and Eddie, in a society dogged by social loneliness?

But Miller tells us in his introduction that these are free men, making a free choice. It may be that they demanded too much from the family, that the strain was too great, that society was at fault in forcing this strain. Nevertheless they were men who did not, in Miller's words, 'settle for half'. Willie, for example, is cruelly treated as a salesman and is driven into obscenity and corruption by his society; still he stands as a man who, eventually at least, knew what he did and who took the consequence as a free choice.

CHAPTER 3

Death of a Salesman

READINGS ON

ARTHUR MILLER

An Introduction to *Death of a Salesman*

Oscar G. Brockett

According to Oscar G. Brockett, the conflicts in *Death of a Salesman* grow out of the tension between Willy Loman's need for material success, love, and admiration, and his confusion over his lack of both material and personal accomplishment. This tension is also the basis for the action of the plot, particularly Willy's psychological flashbacks, in which past and present flow together. Brockett explains how Miller explores the beliefs of Willy's family: Linda, his wife, who loves Willy without questioning his actions; and Biff and Happy, his sons, who are tormented by the mixed values they have learned from Willy. In developing all his characters, Miller concentrates on their social and psychological attitudes. The effective use of mood music and a nonrealistic stage setting enhance the confused psychological state of the characters.

Oscar G. Brockett worked and wrote at Indiana University. In addition to his book *The Theatre*, he has written extensively about American theater, including *A Bibliographical Guide to Research in Speech and Dramatic Art*.

Death of a Salesman explores Willy Loman's obsessive desire to succeed. Willy wants to be recognized, liked, and admired. It is his perplexity over the gulf between his accomplishment and his ideal that precipitates the play's action. Success as Willy conceives it, however, is largely material, for to be well liked and to be materially successful are inextricably linked in his mind.

Because material success seems so necessary to Willy, he believes that his sons cannot love him if he is not successful. Love becomes an item to be bought rather than something to be freely given. Willie has also conditioned his sons to believe that they do not deserve respect unless they are successful on his terms. It is only when Willy understands that Biff loves him, even though both are failures, that he achieves a degree of insight. It is too late to change the course of events, but he goes to his death more nearly at peace than at any time in the play.

The conflicts, then, arise from tensions between the passion for success and the need to be loved and understood. Miller has used two characters to represent the poles between which Willy is pulled. Uncle Ben, Willy's brother, epitomizes material success, while Linda, Willy's wife, represents love given without question or conditions. Willy's dilemma grows out of his unconscious assumption that success is necessary before love is possible.

Many have seen in *Death of a Salesman* a condemnation of American business. Miller has stated that he did not have such a purpose in mind and the play largely bears him out. Charley, a businessman, is one of the most admirable characters in the play and the one who has most nearly achieved success in both private and business life. Charley has never worried about being "a success," however, while Willy has thought of little else. Willy has condoned petty stealing, lying, and cheating so long as they lead toward his goals. His failure, therefore, does not result from being a salesman, but from the means he has used to get ahead. His failure in business is important only because it reflects his failure as a father, husband, and human being.

THE PLOT AND STRUCTURE

Miller has said that he originally conceived the action of *Death of a Salesman* within Willy's mind and that Willy's psychological state dictated the structure of the play. This is only partially true since Willy does not participate in several scenes and could know nothing of them. These exceptions, however, take place in the present; those scenes which go backward in time invariably grow out of Willy's psychological associations.

The present action occurs during a twenty-four-hour period (with the exception of the funeral), but the scenes from the past range over twenty years. Past and present flow together as Willy tries to find the answers to his questions: Why have I failed? Where did I go wrong? What is the secret of success?

It is interesting to compare Miller's play with works from earlier periods. Both *Death of a Salesman* and *Oedipus the King* involve a search into the past to find the roots of present evils. The scenes in *Oedipus the King*, however, are all drawn from the present and the past is revealed only through narration; *Death of a Salesman*, on the other hand, uses Willy's anxieties to transport the audience backward in time to witness scenes. As in *Faust*, there is a search for the meaning of life, but whereas Faust goes forward in time to find fulfillment, Willy goes backward in time to seek the causes of his failure. *Death of a Salesman* also recalls medieval drama in its use of a simultaneous setting and in the complete fluidity of time.

The only unusual structural feature of *Death of a Salesman* is the flashback technique, for otherwise it is organized conventionally in terms of exposition, preparation, complications, climax, obligatory scene, and resolution. Each flashback is carefully introduced by wandering talk, offstage voices, sound effects, music, or some similar cue. Most productions of the play have also used changes in lighting to lead the audience from the present to the past. The flashbacks are carefully engineered so that each reveals only a small part of the past. The outline gradually emerges but is incomplete until the climactic moment.

In *Death of a Salesman* psychological realism has replaced external realism and a greater freedom in dramatic structure has resulted. Although many of the scenes materialize out of Willy's mind and are treated only in fragmentary form, the aim remains much the same as that which moved Ibsen—to depict with fidelity a contemporary situation.

By far the most important character in *Death of a Salesman* is Willy Loman. Biff serves as a strong secondary interest, since the major issues of the play are worked out between him and Willy.

Willy, now sixty-three years old, is on the verge of a physical and psychological breakdown. All his life, he has been trying to sell himself; he has lied both to himself and to others out of a desire to believe that he is a success. Recent developments, however, have forced him to see that actually he is a failure. Yet he cannot see where he has taken the wrong path.

Willy is tired, puzzled, touchy, quick to get angry, ready to hope; he cajoles his sons, offers advice when it is unwanted;

he is always looking for the secret that will "open doors." Above all, he is dominated by the ideal of success, which he tries to instill in his sons as well.

THE IDEAL SALESMAN

Willy Loman's hero is a salesman named David Singleman, who epitomizes Willy's naive and tragic belief that success is a matter of "drumming merchandise" and being well liked. In this excerpt from Death of a Salesman, *Loman tells his boss, Howard, about the well-liked Singleman.*

His name was Dave Singleman. And he was eighty-four years old, and he'd drummed merchandise in thirty-one states. And old Dave, he'd go up to his room, y'understand, put on his green velvet slippers—I'll never forget—and pick up his phone and call the buyers, and without ever leaving his room, at the age of eighty-four, he made his living. And when I saw that, I realized that selling was the greatest career a man could want. 'Cause what could be more satisfying than to be able to go, at the age of eighty-four, into twenty or thirty different cities, and pick up a phone, and be remembered and loved and helped by so many different people? Do you know? when he died—and by the way he died the death of a salesman, in his green velvet slippers in the smoker of the New York, New Haven and Hartford, going into Boston—when he died, hundreds of salesmen and buyers were at his funeral. Things were sad on a lotta trains for months after that. *He stands up. Howard has not looked at him.* In those days there was personality in it, Howard. There was respect, and comradeship, and gratitude in it.

Uncle Ben personifies success, and in many ways is merely an extension of Willy's personality. He represents the mystery of success, for he has gone into the jungle and come out rich; he has been to far-away and dangerous places and thus he gives a romantic aura to success. Ben also implies that success is bound up with the "law of the jungle," with shady deals and quick-wittedness.

Willy, however, wants to triumph on his own terms—as a salesman who is liked by everybody. Therefore, he can never completely accept Ben's advice just as he can never give up Ben's ideal. This division is at the root of Willy's character and is seen even in his death, which is a final attempt to achieve material gain and the gratitude of his family simultaneously. He is both a pathetic and a powerful figure.

Biff is thirty-four years old but still adolescent in his attitudes. He is irresponsible, a wanderer, and incapable of happiness because of the sense of guilt aroused in him by Willy. From Willy he learned early that the way to success lies through lying, stealing, and powerful acquaintances. But the lure of success has been short-circuited in Biff by his disillusionment with Willy, dating from the discovery of his father's unfaithfulness to his mother. Consequently, Biff rebels against success, flouts authority, and enjoys hurting his father.

Biff has his admirable side, nevertheless, for he tries to face the truth, and he has a sense of moral responsibility which his brother, Happy, is totally lacking. It is Biff who finally makes his father see the truth as they both come to understand that love is a gift freely bestowed rather than something earned through material success. Miller gives no indication of what the future holds for Biff, but it will no doubt be more peaceful than the past.

Linda understands from the beginning what Willy and Biff learn during the play: love has no conditions. She knows all there is to know about Willy, but she loves him, accepts him, and fights fiercely for him, even against her own sons. Her sense of decency and rightness makes her put Willy above everyone, for to her it is not a question of whether Willy has earned love and respect—his right to them is unquestioned. Because she loves so unconditionally, Linda cannot understand why Willy commits suicide or why the boys have turned out as they have. Success holds no magic for Linda. She fears Ben and his lures. It is only because of Biff that Willy eventually begins to see the appeal of Linda's view.

Happy has inherited the worst of Willy's traits without the saving possibility of love. He is entirely selfish and unfeeling; lying and cheating are integral parts of his nature. He is a materialist and sensualist beyond redemption, but devoid of Ben's vision and strength.

Charley and Bernard have succeeded where Willy and Biff have failed; thus, their principal function in the play is to serve as contrasts. Charley says that he has succeeded because he has never been passionately dedicated to anything. Yet the play shows that Charley is dedicated to being a good man, as opposed to being a success in Willy's terms. Although unaware of his dedication, Charley's unconscious commitment to *human* above *material* factors is the key to his happiness, just as the reverse is the key to Willy's failure.

Many have seen in Howard an indictment of the "businessman's morality." Miller has denied this and has said that Howard is a man of common sense and that he acts as he must. More importantly for the play, however, Howard spurs Willy on in his search for an answer. In real-life terms it might have been more humane for Howard to find a place for Willy in the home office, but in terms of dramatic action his decision is necessary to make Willy face himself more completely. In constructing his characters, Miller has concentrated upon sociological and psychological attitudes; other details have been cut away. Miller's success in creating convincing figures is indicated by the general tendency of audiences to see in the play a clear reflection of modern society.

STAGING AND THE USE OF SOUND

Miller's ideas about staging *Death of a Salesman* are clearly indicated in the script. The continuous presence of the house helps to establish the convention that the flashbacks are fragments of the past and to make clear the simultaneity of the past and the present in Willy's mind.

Miller has stated that the motion picture version of *Death of a Salesman* was not successful in large part because of the overly realistic depiction of the settings used for the flashback scenes. He believes that in this way the emphasis was shifted from the psychological conflict in Willy's mind to the physical background. The fragmentary and schematic setting specified by Miller eliminates many illusionistic details. It is entirely in keeping with the dramatic techniques used in the play.

Sound has also been used effectively. Music helps to set the mood and to mark transitions to flashback scenes. Ben has his own special music, played each time he appears; honky-tonk music accompanies Willy's scenes with the Other Woman; music helps to set the locale of the restaurant scene. The method by which Willy commits suicide is made clear only through the offstage sound of a car driving away.

Although audiences have accepted as realistic the fragmentary setting and novel staging conventions and have never been puzzled by them, the realism of *Death of a Salesman* has been modified by cutting away the surface so that the inner reality may be seen more clearly. Miller's methods are representative of the way in which realism is practiced in present-day theatre.

Death of a Salesman as Tragedy

Richard J. Foster

Richard J. Foster suggests that any staging of *Death of a Salesman* eventually leads the audience to the question, Is it a tragedy? When the play opened in 1949, dissatisfied critics frequently accused Miller of writing an "incomplete" tragedy. Within weeks, the playwright published a response in which he emphatically defended *Death of a Salesman* as a modern tragedy and Willy Loman as a modern tragic hero.

After defining the traditional view of tragedy, Foster outlines Arthur Miller's own definition. The playwright argues that because his drama captures the feeling or essence of the tragic, *Death of a Salesman* is no less a tragedy than Shakespeare's *Hamlet*.

Foster disagrees, arguing that *Death of a Salesman* is more Willy's prolonged cry for help than Willy's tragedy. Willy Loman is a dreamer caught in a society dominated by machines, competition, and the principle of getting ahead at any cost. Willy's capacity for love, self-respect, and individuality is stunted by circumstances, and, therefore, the protagonist must be seen as a pathetic victim rather than a tragic hero.

Richard J. Foster, professor of English, lectured at the University of Minnesota, Minneapolis, on modern literature and criticism.

Sooner or later most discussions of the merits of Arthur Miller's *Death of a Salesman* turn to the question of the possibility of modern tragedy. Given the conditions of the modern world, the question runs, is it possible to write true tragedy in our time? Of course the very asking of the question sounds the negative. . . . And Miller himself, in response to commentators who have denied that *Salesman* is a tragedy, has vigorously affirmed, in an essay called "Tragedy and the Common Man," the right of his play, and the matter it is made of, to the epithet *tragic*. That both critic and playwright care so strongly about how the words *tragic* and *tragedy* are to be applied shows at the very least that the words carry a rather heavy charge of positive value. But there is also a theoretical question behind the question of value, and the differences between Miller and his critics can be accounted for at least partially on the basis of the difference between their "theories" of tragedy.

A TRADITIONAL VIEW OF TRAGEDY

To put the matter very simply, Arthur Miller has a very general or very loose and vague theory of tragedy, or perhaps no clear theory at all, while the critics have a fairly definite one derived from a couple of thousand years of literary tradition. The traditional view of tragedy, founded very largely upon the principles of Aristotle and the practice of Sophocles and Shakespeare, assumes at least two prior essentials to be inherent in the materials of any tragic action. First, the hero must have "stature": this means that while he must in some way represent the general human condition, he must also be larger and grander than the norm—certainly in the inherent fineness and depth and energy of his mind and character, and perhaps also in his exterior societal role—so that his fall will have deep emotional consequence for the audience. Second, the world in which the tragic hero acts must be sensed as bounded or permeated by some meaningful and larger-than-human order—call it a Moral Order, or the Natural Law, or Providence, or even Fate—which he in some way challenges or violates and which correspondingly exacts, but not without some sense of ultimate justice in the exaction, the tragic hero's life in consequence of that violation. The first part of this formula, the requirement of "stature" in the tragic hero, Miller's play obviously fails to live up to. Willy Loman is a childish and stupid human being, and his societal role of salesman is of only very minor consequence. And since one of the thematic intentions of the play is to present the picture of a world in which there can be no moral appeal to an order more profound than those of commerce and the machine, *Salesman* obviously cannot meet the second requirement either.

So by the test of tradition, *Death of a Salesman*, whatever else it may be, is no tragedy. But wait, Miller seems to say in "Tragedy and the Common Man," by the test of *feeling* it *is* tragedy. "The tragic feeling," he writes, "is evoked when we are in the presence of a character who is ready to lay down his life, if need be, to secure one thing—his sense of personal dignity." He mentions Orestes, Hamlet, Medea, and Macbeth as examples, and goes on to say that "in the tragic view the need of man to wholly realize himself is the only fixed star, and whatever hedges his nature and lowers it is ripe for attack and examination." Miller is affirming, then, a continuity in tragedy that is not dependent upon historical accidents: what counts is the tragic *sense*, not the mechanical details of an abstract formula for the tragic. In spite of history, Miller is saying, in *felt* significance *Death of a Salesman* is just as much a tragedy as Sophocles' *Electra* or Shakespeare's *Hamlet*. Putting aside formulas and abstractions, let us examine it on its own grounds—not only in the light of the *kind* of play it is ("bourgeois tragedy"), . . . but also in the more universal light of the truth and depth and integrity that we expect from any piece of real literature, regardless of its time or type.

Two things will strike us when we consider Miller's focal character, Willy Loman, and both of them are in Miller's favor. First, we cannot miss the force of Willy's imagination, the energy of his language, the ferocity of his hope and rage. (Miller uses the word "mercurial" to sum this up in his stage directions.) We *know* that Willy is a pathetic fool, but we nevertheless *feel* him vividly as a vital human being. He may be mediocre, even barbaric, but he is not dull. And second, we cannot miss Willy's failure always to translate imagination and feeling into effective action. His continual inconsistencies, for example: Biff is both a "lazy bum" and "hard worker" to Willy in Act I, and in Act II Willy's advice to Biff on conducting his interview with Bill Oliver is that he should both "talk as little as possible" and "start off with a couple of . . . good stories to lighten things up." Willy says of himself at one point, and all in one breath, "I'm very well liked in Hartford. You know, the trouble is, Linda, people just don't seem to take to me." Willy's great intensity provides a recognizable touch, at least, of something like "stature." And perhaps his incoherence of mind and will resembles the "flaw" of nature or judgment usually borne by the traditional tragic hero. Like Hamlet—or at least the Hamlet that some of the critics think they see—Willy's personal tragedy is that he is inherently unable to bring himself to take the rational action necessary to save himself and put his world in order. But unlike Hamlet, Willy seems to have suffered his tragedy all his life. With reflections of the past playing continually over the present, Miller's play focuses on the end of that life when, ironically, the last opportunity for creative action remaining to Willy is the opportunity to destroy himself.

Death of a Salesman is a play remarkably lacking in action—which is not to say that it is a bad play for that reason. This lack of action, this continual dispersion of motive in Willy, is of course part of the play's theme. Intensity of feeling plus confusion of intellect yields paralysis of will. Willy's inability to act in any coherent way, an inability that the flashbacks show us is not confined only to Willy's old age, seems to be related directly to his inability to see the truth, or to his inability to distinguish between illusion and actuality, or to harmonize his dreams with his responsibilities. Charley says to Willy, after Willy has been in effect fired by Howard, "The only thing you got in this world is what you can sell. And the funny thing is that you're a salesman, and you don't know that." Charley means that Willy is suffering because he is looking for a deeply human fulfillment in an activity which is conditioned not by what is human, but by goods and cash.

WILLY'S FLAWED DREAMS

Charley himself sees the "facts" of business and selling as they are, and he is thereby able to keep his practical sense and his humanity sharply distinguished, in balance, intact. But Willy, perhaps a greater personality than either Charley or Bernard, however much more childish and unintelligent he may be than they, has an incurable vision. It is a vision that Charley knows cannot be realized in selling, for it implies creativity, heroism, beauty, and wholeness: the creativity of Willy's father, the free and wandering inventor; the heroism of Ben, who tamed two continents and made them serve him; the beauty of Biff at seventeen—"a young god, Hercules ... and the sun all around him"—receiving the cheers of the crowd at Ebbets Field; the wholeness of Dave Singleman, who, like an old king full of honor, could simply

pick up the phone in his hotel room and command the respect and love of hundreds at the other end. Biff, who functions in the play as an amplification or reflection of Willy's
problems, has been nurtured on Willy's dreams too. But he
has been forced to see the truth. And it is the truth—his father's cheap philandering—in its impact on a nature already
weakened by a diet of illusion that in turn paralyzes him.
Biff and Willy are two versions of the idealist, or "dreamer"
may be a better word, paralyzed by reality: Biff by the effects
of disillusionment, Willy by the effects of the illusions themselves. This is how they sum themselves up at the end of the
play, just before Willy's suicide: "Pop!" Biff cries, "I'm a dime
a dozen, and so are you!" "I am not a dime a dozen!" Willy
answers in rage. "I am Willy Loman, and you are Biff
Loman!" And the tragedy—if it *is* tragedy—is that they are
both right.

But why is it that Willy and Biff, both of them meant by
Miller to be taken as men of potential, must be paralyzed
and defeated? It seems to be a matter partly of psychological
accident. Willy never had a real father, and his hard preda-
tory older brother became his father-substitute. "Never fight
fair with a stranger" was Ben's wisdom. And his faith—
"When I was seventeen I walked into the jungle, and when I
was twenty-one I walked out. And by God I was rich!" It
seems also to be a matter partly of historical accident: times
have changed. If ever there were days when essentially
human values and loyalties prevailed in the world of selling,
those days passed with old Dave Singleman and Willy's former boss. The business world is now run by cold young ma-
terialists like Howard, and though a wise realist like Charley
may survive, there is no place in it for the all-too human
dreamer and vulgarian, Willy Loman.

Psychology, history—these lead us to the third and most
important cause of Willy's suffering, the great evil, the great
villain of most modern writing in the realist vein—Society.
Keeping in mind traditional tragedy and how it brings the
audience's attention to bear on the relation between the
tragic hero and the moral order implied in the background
of his action, we see that Willy, unlike the traditional tragic
hero, is meant to be seen as greater and better, at least in potential, than the world that destroys him. While the traditional tragic hero is felt to be in some way responsible to a
moral order larger than himself, and fulfills that responsi-

bility, sometimes with the overtones of sacrifice, even of "atonement," in the event, by losing his life, the hero of bourgeois tragedy tends to be better than the order—not a moral order now, but a merely mechanical social order—and is victimized by it. Willy Loman is potentially better than his world in that he has at least incipient values that are better than the world's values. Society's guilt, as it is projected in *Death of a Salesman*, lies in its not making available ways and means for a man like Willy to implement and realize those values, and in dooming him thus to frustration, paralysis, and ultimately destruction as a human being.

The values that seem to be represented in Willy, the "good" values that function in the play as implicit criticisms of society's "bad" values, are the familiar romantic ones: nature, freedom, and the body; free self-expression and self-realization; individualism and the simple life. Nature and the simple life are supposed to be announced in the play's opening flute music, which, Miller tells us in a stage direction, speaks "of grass and trees and the horizon." Willy's memories of the wisteria and elms around the house when the boys were young, his vague dream of having a farm in his old age, his symbolic attempts to plant seeds in the night, and Biff's rhapsodies about the bare-chested life and young colts and the western plains, are all overshadowed and threatened by the encroaching bulwarks of apartment houses and the costly and complicated machines that sap one's resources and won't perform their functions. Willy's life is a continuum of futile worry, and his garden is a shadowed and sterile plot where the life-giving sun can no longer get in. Though Biff was a "young god" and Willy a spokesman for toughness, Society seems to have stifled these goods too: Willy has become soft and fat: Biff and Happy, inhabitants of a world where "getting ahead of the next fella" is the prime goal, find their strength and energy turning into bullying; and all of them display a mistaken and self-defeating contempt for the mind.

THE FAILURES OF THE LOMAN FAMILY

Another category of value against which society militates has to do with the feelings, with love, with deep and full and natural human relationship. The real capacities for love of both Willy and his boys disperses itself in meaningless and trivial philanderings. Biff and Happy yearn fruitlessly to run a

WILLY LACKS HEROIC STATURE

In his introduction to Death of a Salesman *in* The Heath Introduction to Drama, *critic Jordan Y. Miller writes that Willy Loman is not a tragic hero. He argues that Willy has been destroyed not by society, but rather by himself.*

Death of a Salesman is not, however, a modern tragedy. Society has not destroyed Willy Loman. Willy Loman has destroyed himself. More precisely, he has destroyed an image of himself in his own imagination of what society is and what the business world expects of him. Nowhere are we permitted to see Willy Loman except through his own eyes. He says he was a great salesman. There is not a shred of evidence. Why has the old refrigerator had to last so many years, the old car so many miles? Willy insists that there are great rewards for what he does and he seems at one time to have reaped them. But we see nothing of substance to support his claims. Willy is a sham, through and through, living on what he thinks he is and what he thinks is right, while all along the young Bernard next door gives the lie to Willy's theories of how to raise a family and how to perform in society. The fact that Bernard can argue before the Supreme Court is incomprehensible to the Willy who could see no purpose in the scholarly bookishness of his next door neighbor's son. And Willy never really sees that Charley is the one who has succeeded, and who has the money to keep Willy alive. How come Willy doesn't have it? . . .

Willy's suicide is not the positive act of tragedy. It is the act of one who still thinks in terms of self-redemption, of being able to "make it up" to those he has done wrong. True, Willy is a man, and maybe he should have some attention paid. But Willy is a very little man in all ways, and while we weep for him and may be deeply moved, he remains with feet of very sticky clay, firmly fastened to the ground, far from the heights demanded of tragedy.

ranch or a business together—the *together* is what is important—and to marry decent girls with, as they put it, "substance," just as Willy dreams of a happy old age with his children and his children's children thriving happily around him. But sterility and disharmony obtain: the boys, growing older, do not marry, and Willy's hopes for his family explode with finality in the chaos of the terrible restaurant scene in Act II. The enemy of love, of course, is society's principle of "success"—getting ahead by competition, which is the impersonal opposite of love. It is significant that Willy's vision of fulfillment is made up of characters who stand alone—Willy's father, Brother Ben, Biff as a public hero, Dave Singleman—characters who have succeeded, who stand not with but above and beyond the rest of humanity, and who do not give love but receive it, and at an impersonal distance, from cheering crowds or from faceless respectful voices at the other ends of telephone lines. This vision, created and enforced by the norms of the competitive, success-centered society that Willy lives in, is a denial of the deeply personal and human capacities for love that are inherent in Willy's nature.

A final set of values implicit in Willy's character, and defeated by the circumstances in which he finds himself, are his unformed impulses toward two of the original American virtues—self-reliance and individualism of spirit. These virtues, implying basic self-sufficiency and personal creativity, *not* domination of others, are perhaps the pure forms underlying the corrupt and destructive societal imperatives of success and getting ahead. Willy has the self-reliant skills of the artisan: he is "good at things," from polishing a car to building a front porch, and we hear of his beloved tools and his dream of using them some day to build a guest house on his dreamed-of farm for his boys and their families to stay in. But self-reliance has collapsed, the tools rust, and Willy has become the futile and pathetic victim of a machine culture. And individualism has been translated and corrupted in Willy into a belief in the jungle value of privilege for the strong: he encourages his boys to steal, and he calls it initiative and their right. . . .

Miller once said in a panel discussion of his play that Willy Loman is "seeking for a kind of ecstasy in life, which the machine civilization deprives people of. He's looking for his selfhood, for his immortal soul, so to speak." I think that most tragic heroes in the tradition were doing something rather different from this—making hazardous decisions and taking action in consequence of them, action that elicited the scrutiny of, perhaps challenged, a greater moral order outside themselves. Miller's statement may explain why *Death of a Salesman* is so little like an action, so much like a prolonged cry—Linda's cry, perhaps, that "attention must be paid." And perhaps it is, very simply, this aim of expressing not an idea, but only an agony that keeps *Death of a Salesman* from being either a "tragedy" or a great piece of literature.

Characterization in *Death of a Salesman*

Edward Murray

Edward Murray asserts that Willy and Biff Loman are well-developed, interesting characters, but the minor players are disappointingly flat. While the audience learns the background, motivation, and flaws of both Willy and Biff, the minor characters are static, single-note supporting players. Linda, for example, is unselfish, Howard is callous, and Bernard is steady. Nevertheless, Murray feels that in general Miller's characterization succeeds within the overall design of the play.

Edward Murray is a professor of English at State University of New York at Brockport. His works include *Clifford Odets: The Thirties and After*, *Ten Film Classics*, and *The Cinematic Imagination: Writers and the Motion Pictures*. Murray is a contributor to *College Language Association Journal* and *Literature/ Film Quarterly*.

Physically, Willy Loman is not described in detail: "He is past sixty years of age, dressed quietly . . . [and] his exhaustion is apparent"; but there is contrast here, for Willy—who stresses "appearances"—is simply not physically "impressive." Sociologically, Willy belongs to the lower-middle class. Dialogue reveals that he is a traveling salesman from Brooklyn, who has averaged seventy to one hundred dollars a week for a period of over thirty years, but to earn such money, Willy must "be at it ten, twelve hours a day." Willy's job has no built-in security against old age. Through dialogue, Miller creates a sense of the past. Willy became a salesman because in the early days selling seemed to possess "comradeship" and real "personality," but selling has changed in thirty years, and Willy cannot adjust to the changes. Not that Willy was ever a great salesman, even in the early days. Actually, Willy would probably have been happier as a carpenter, although in the play he takes a superior stance toward "mere" carpentering. Willy seems to have had little education; his father was always on the move, "he'd toss the whole family into the wagon, and then he'd drive the team right across the country." There is no religion in Willy's life, no philosophical system to sustain him, and no political convictions to absorb or direct his energy. Willy believes everything he reads in the newspaper—even the advertisements. Willy Loman is "low-man": the alienated, hypersensitive, urbanized cipher of modern society. Psychologically, Willy has many traits. He appreciates nature and he is often nostalgic. He is both dependent on Linda and domineering toward her. (He reveals the same pattern with Charley.) Willy is persistent—he "can't walk away." He is clearly gullible. His father, who is held up as a "real man," actually abandoned his family to search for gold in Alaska and this abandonment has left Willy with deep feelings of insecurity. Consequently, Willy feels the need to overcompensate by being "number-one." His dominant trait, then, is a restless ambition for "success." Willy tends to exaggerate; his moods swing abruptly. Although Willy has been sexually unfaithful to Linda, he is no callous profligate. He feels deep remorse. Clearly, then, Willy has a tender conscience. This sensitivity is also manifest in Willy's frustration over not having attained his idealized image of himself—and over Biff's not having attained Willy's idealized image of Biff. The inner contradiction that drives Willy to self-destruction is the need to prove his worth against the fear that he has failed as both a father and a salesman: "I am not a dime a dozen! I am Willy Loman, and you are Biff Loman!"

BIFF LOMAN

Biff is described in this manner:

> Biff is two years older than his brother Happy [that is, thirty-four], well built, but in these days bears a worn air and seems less self-assured. He has succeeded less, and his dreams are stronger and less acceptable than Happy's.

After his days of high school football glory, things changed for Biff:

> I spent six or seven years after high school trying to work myself up. Shipping clerk, salesman, business of one kind or an-

other. And it's a measly manner of existence . . . when all you really desire is to be outdoors. . . . And still—that's how you build a future.

Dialogue also illuminates Biff's hopes for the future: "with a ranch I could do the work I like and still be something"; it also reveals how Biff comes to reject that "something":

What am I doing in [Oliver's] office, making a contemptuous, begging fool of myself, when all I want is out [West], waiting for me the minute I say I know who I am!

Biff is rich in traits: he is moody; he is a petty, compulsive thief—which suggests that Biff feels unloved for what he is in himself; he is spiteful; he is proud; he is self-deceived; he suffers from self-contempt. Unlike Willy, however, Biff has the capacity to face the truth about himself. Biff's dominant trait, in fact, is his restless search for self-identity. His inner contradiction is precisely his ambivalent attitude toward his father. Thus, he tells the girl in the cafe that Willy is

---

MILLER REFLECTS ON HIS FEMALE CHARACTERS

When asked by interviewer Matthew C. Roudané to describe his female characters in the summer 1985 issue of Michigan Quarterly Review, *Arthur Miller defends his heroines as less passive and sentimental than they have been seen. Although they are often peripheral to the action, Miller believes his female characters are psychologically complex.*

MR: Reflecting upon Kate Keller in *All My Sons*, Elizabeth Proctor in *The Crucible*, and, say, Linda Loman in *Death of a Salesman*, could you discuss the roles the women play in your drama?

AM: A production of *All My Sons* was on in England two years ago and was directed by Michael Blakemore, a very fine director, who had never seen it here. He saw Kate (Rosemary Harris) as a woman using the truth as a weapon against the man who had harmed their son. Kate Keller is pretty damn sure when the play begins that, in the widest sense of the word, Joe was "responsible" for the deaths of the Air Force men. She's both warning him not to go down the road that his older son is beckoning him to go, and rather ambiguously destroying him with her knowledge of his crime. She sees the horror most clearly because she was a partner to it without having committed it. There's a sinister side to her, in short. This actress caught it beautifully. The production was "dark" because of her performance of

a fine, troubled prince. A hardworking unappreciated prince. A pal . . . a good companion. Always for his boys.

But he tells Willy:

> I never got anywhere because you blew me so full of hot air I could never stand taking orders from anybody! That's whose fault it is!

The contradiction results in Biff's paralyzing confusion: "I don't know—what I'm supposed to want."

MINOR CHARACTERS

None of the other characters in *Salesman* has the complexity of Willy and Biff. All of them are very nearly dominated by a single trait: Happy is selfish, Linda is unselfish, Ben is confident, Howard is callous, Bernard is steady, and Charley is "mature." Similarly, the minor characters are static. Are Willy and Biff static? Willy certainly arrives at a mild condemnation of selling when, in regard to his suicide plan and

---

the mother who is usually regarded as ancillary, which she is not.

MR: Perhaps, then, there's more complexity to your female characters than critics have generally recognized.

AM: Critics generally see them as far more passive than they are. When I directed *Salesman* in China I had Linda "in action." She's not just sitting around. She's the one who knows from the beginning of the play that Willy's trying to kill himself. She's got the vital information all the time. Linda sustains the illusion because that's the only way Willy can be sustained. At the same time any cure or change is impossible in Willy. Ironically she's helping to guarantee that Willy will never recover from his illusion. She has to support it; she has no alternative, given his nature and hers.

MR: So, in this context, Linda is supporting what Ibsen would call a "vital lie."

AM: That's right. The women characters in my plays are very complex. They've been played somewhat sentimentally, but that isn't the way they were intended. There is a more sinister side to the women characters in my plays. These women are of necessity auxiliaries to the action, which is carried by the male characters. But they both receive the benefits of the male's mistakes and protect his mistakes in crazy ways. They are forced to do that. So the females are victims as well.

the resultant insurance money, he tells Ben: "This would not be another damned-fool appointment. . . ." He also comes to see that Biff truly loves him. Basically, however, Willy remains the same throughout the play—and this, of course, would seem to be Miller's point. Character growth—William Archer preferred "disclosure"—is only a means to an end. We can believe in static Willy in a way we cannot believe in "jumping" Joe Keller in *All My Sons.* Biff, on the other hand, definitely grows, for he achieves a number of insights that culminate in a major development in self-awareness. Biff sees, for example, that he was self-deceived about Oliver; he sees how all the Lomans have been self-deceived; and he stops his "spiteful" behavior toward Willy and relinquishes the "phony dream," thus accepting the "reality" of himself.

It has been said that Biff, not Willy, is the protagonist in *Salesman.* If we consider the action of the play, however, and not preconceived and arbitrary criteria, it is easy to see why Willy, not Biff, is the protagonist. It is Willy who forces the conflict; Willy who cannot surrender his "dream"; Willy who will not allow Biff to rest in his "failure"; Willy who asks Howard for a job in New York; Willy who is unfaithful to Linda; Willy who borrows money from Charley; Willy who pursues Ben for the "answer"; and Willy who destroys himself in order to be "number-one."

Finally, the unity of opposites in the play is binding. Compromise is impossible between Willy and Biff, both men being what they are and desiring different things. (Compromise is also impossible between Willy and the "system"— what Willy wants, even only a "little salary," and what Howard will give him—"I can't take blood from a stone"— are opposed.) What makes the unity binding is the simple fact that Willy "can't walk away" from Biff. (Willy, it is true, could take a job from Charley, but he is too proud to admit defeat—and it is his pride that drives him to suicide.)

DEPTH OF CHARACTERIZATION

The above discussion should make plain that Willy and Biff are three-dimensional characters. Structurally, as we have seen, dialogue performs its office through expert exposition and foreshadowing. Here, in terms of character, dialogue is made to reveal as much of the past, present, and future of Willy and Biff as is necessary for a proper understanding of the action. In short, dialogue in *Salesman* is extremely functional. One reason why Willy is more alive than Joe Keller is the fact that dialogue is more specific about Willy—we learn more about the salesman, such as, his important childhood environment (which helps us to understand his adult behavior) or that he lives in Brooklyn, New York (which helps us to place him within a concrete context and also to make allowances for his speech patterns). The more we know about Willy, the more interest we have in his fate. The fact that Miller starts the point of attack with Willy already an attempted suicide, with the focus steadily on Willy as the protagonist, and with Willy's inner contradictions continually on view, permits us to believe in Willy and his death in a way that was impossible in the case of Joe Keller.

There is no denying, however, that something is lacking in the minor characters. One might argue that Willy and Biff are at the center of things, that they are sufficiently delineated, and that there is no necessity for the other characters to be fully drawn. There is some truth in such an argument, for every play requires flat characters. Charley, Bernard, Howard, and Ben are perhaps "there" enough for the parts they are to enact. Critic Eric Bentley has asked whether Ben is "more than a sentimental motif?" Since Ben is seen in the play by Willy alone, and since Willy is sentimental about Ben, the answer to Bentley seems obvious. But Bentley's charge that Willy's marriage is not "*there* for us to inspect and understand down to its depths" is less easy to counter. Although Miller's concern is with Willy and Biff, not Willy and Linda, the fact remains that Linda is more flat than would seem either desirable or necessary. To a lesser extent, the same criticism might be scored against Happy. A play, however, is not judged by its characters alone, for every element in a play is part of a total design, and characters are evaluated in respect to how well they contribute to that design.

Loneliness in
Death of a Salesman

Winifred L. Dusenbury

Winifred L. Dusenbury sees Willy Loman as distraught with loneliness. Willy's sense of separation
results from his shallow vision of success and his
failure to understand basic moral principles. Dusenbury emphasizes the point that Willy is personally
responsible for failing to develop his talents, nurture
friendships, and connect with his family.

Winifred L. Dusenbury is a professor of English
at the University of Florida, Gainesville. Her works
include (under the name of Winifred Dusenbury
Frazer) *Love as Death in The Iceman Cometh* and
Emma Goldman and The Iceman Cometh. She contributes articles on modern drama to professional
journals and magazines.

In another of the most popular American dramas of recent
years, *Death of a Salesman*, is to be found exemplification of
what sociologist David Riesman calls the other-directed individual, who, living in hope of the approval of his peers, is
seldom free of a diffuse anxiety lest this approval be with-
held. Willy Loman, whose aim in life is to be not just "liked,"
but "well liked," is too pitifully wrong to be tragic, perhaps,
but he represents a failure typical of the times. As Riesman
points out, the economy of the country, especially in the past
few decades, has given particular emphasis to consuming,
for production is able to take care of itself. But to increase
consumption, more and better salesmen are needed. In
Willy Loman, boxed in his Brooklyn house by towering
apartment buildings, trying in vain to grow a few seeds in
the darkness of the shadows, is portrayed the lonely traveling salesman, who is not successful because he holds that to
be "well liked" is the *aim* of living rather than the *result* of
unselfish thoughtfulness of others.

WILLY LOMAN'S LONELINESS

"I was lonely, I was terribly lonely," Willy says to Biff in explaining the woman "buyer" in his hotel room. Wonderingly, on the verge of tears, Willy says to his old neighbor, "Charley, you're the only friend I got. Isn't that a remarkable thing?" To Linda, he says, "On the road—on the road I want to grab you sometimes and just kiss the life outa you. 'Cause I get so lonely—...." No doubt Willy as a salesman is susceptible to a kind of loneliness which to men in other work might not be so keen, for he is "a man way out there in the blue, riding on a smile and a shoeshine." But Willy's isolation and failure come about because, as Biff perceptively says after his death, "He had the wrong dreams. All, all wrong." To see the surface of life was his undoing. Perceiving that the men who made good were well liked (for their money if nothing else) he assumed that to be well liked was to make good and that making good was the end of all living.

On the last day of his life he still did not see beyond that. He recognized his failure in himself and in his sons, but even at the end of his life he had no vision of the truth. His final words to the rich brother he imagines stands before him—"Ben! Ben, where do I . . . ? Ben, how do I . . . ?"—indicate that he had no insight of where he had gone wrong. Willy's lonesomeness is of his own making, but it is of his times as well, for a century ago there was a chance to own a sunny lot large enough to raise a garden, and a man was likely to be in creatively productive work. The play's popularity is testimony to the effectiveness of its characterizations and its dramaturgy, but most of all perhaps to its dramatization of the plight of many Americans today. . . .

WILLY'S DISTORTED MORAL PRINCIPLES

The play, which might be called "Failure of an American" as well as *Death of a Salesman,* conveys the idea that, although Willy might be representative of many, it is nonetheless his own failure—not that of America—which brings his downfall. If many are in the same dilemma, the place to look for a solution is not in society, but in themselves. Willy's affair with a woman on his selling trips is excusable, at the worst a sordid reminder of the flesh in mankind. Not so, his encouraging Biff to steal the football; not so, his boasting of the expensive lumber his boys have taken from a nearby lot; not so, his flouting the integrity of the school in proclaiming that the principal would not dare flunk an athlete like Biff; not so, his thanking "Almighty God" that his sons are built like Adonises because they will therefore be well liked.

No wonder Willy feels "kind of temporary" about himself. His sense of honesty is badly distorted, and his recognition of the values of integrity, truth, and responsibility is very slight. His loneliness results partly from his inability to understand the moral principles, which to a man like his neighbor, Charley, are innate. It is certain, too, that he exaggerates the extent of the hard work which he has devoted to the New England territory. Personality, in his thinking, has always been more important than work. Like Willy, the successful American from the time of the pioneers has had grandiose visions of success, but unlike Willy he has labored to bring them to reality.

WILLY'S DESIRE FOR FRIENDSHIP

The pitiful thing about Willy is his belief that, more than for wealth or fame, he longs for friendship. All his dreams are of friendship and comradeship, and his thoughts of the past include the happy relationship between himself and his boys. His memories of the 84-year-old salesman, who was so successful that he called his buyers to come to his hotel room, revolve not upon the money he made, but upon the friends he had.

> 'Cause what could be more satisfying than to be able to go, at the age of eighty-four, into twenty or thirty different cities, and pick up a phone, and be remembered and loved and helped by so many different people?

In those days, recalls Willy, there was comradeship in selling. The actual fact of his not being able to make a living at the end of his life did not hurt Willy half so much as the fact that nobody knew him. His final sacrifice was made so that Linda might have the insurance money, but also in hopes that hundreds of imagined friends would come to his funeral from "Maine, Massachusetts, Vermont and New Hampshire."

Throughout his life Willy had compensated for his failure by dreams of personal popularity, the success of his sons, and recognition by his company. Finally forced to acknowledge that reality has clashed irrevocably with his dreams, Willy at the end makes a fruitless but valiant effort to save himself by feverishly planting carrot, beet, and lettuce seeds in his dark back yard. Even in his distraught state he recognizes that if he can make a little plant grow, he may be saved. With suicide strongly in his mind, getting close to the dirt may make him want to live. If seeds will grow, he still can grow. Although he has sometimes had idealistic dreams of natural scenes of beautiful growing trees and grass in the New England countryside, and of lilac and wisteria and peonies around his own house, he now turns to the soil, not sentimentally, but with a terrible hunger for reality. Imagination has failed him, but in the earth there is still hope—not dreams, but food. It is too late, however. Willy senses that his company does not know him; his buyers do not know him; his sons do not know him; a heartbreaking loneliness tells him it is time to die.

An analysis of the play from the point of view of the function of the theme of loneliness which runs through it must be made with Arthur Miller's statement about the play in mind: "the remembered thing about 'Salesman' is really the basic situation in which these people find themselves." The situation is of importance in itself, not as a background for the growth of character or for dramatic action. The situation in which a father is separated from his sons, and a mother from both sons and father in trying to mediate between them, is basic to the play. How the family became separated is the story of the play. Told in flashbacks as they come to Willy's mind, the incidents reveal the deleterious effect upon the family relationship of the false ideals which Willy holds and instills in his sons. As the play is constructed, Willy has reached a state of isolation in the first scene, which results in his suicide in the last. In between, the explanation for his plight is revealed in remembered incidents. The situation itself is not dramatic, but the revelation of the causes for it is very dramatic.

WILLY'S SEPARATION FROM BIFF

Many of these revelatory incidents are plays in miniature with a rising action and climax of their own. For example, the series of incidents which lead up to the climactic scene in which Biff finds his father with a cheap woman in his hotel room are all dramatic. In the opening scene Willy becomes irate when Linda mentions that Biff is finding himself. "Not finding yourself at the age of thirty-four is a disgrace," he shouts. With illogical contradiction in his reasoning with regard to Biff, he continues, "The trouble is he's lazy, god-dammit!" and a few speeches later he surprisingly adds, "And such a hard worker. There's one thing about Biff—he's not lazy." Willy's irritation toward Biff for his antagonism carries over into the conversation with Linda in a series of contra-dictions: "Why do you get American when I like Swiss? . . . Why am I always being contradicted?" Later he says, "Why don't you open a window in here, for God's sake?" She replies, "They're all open, dear." Complaining about the sti-fling neighborhood in which they live, he says, "there's more people now." To Linda's gentle reply, "I don't think there's more people," he yells, "There's more people! That what's ru-ining this country." This first scene, in which it is made ob-vious that an intense feeling has split father and son, lays the groundwork for the following ones concerning Biff and Willy.

The next scene in this series takes place between the mother and sons, who have been wakened by Willy's mut-tering and have come downstairs to talk to their mother. She berates Biff for his lack of consideration for his father. Biff replies: "He threw me out of the house, remember that." Linda asks, "Why did he do that? I never knew why." Biff's explanation indicates the bitterness of his feeling toward his father. "Because I know he's a fake and he doesn't like any-body around who knows! . . . Just don't lay it all at my feet. It's between me and him. . . ." It is an unusual situation in which a mother does not know why a father has thrown out their son. The question raised is still unsettled as the scene rises to a pitch through a happy interlude of planning for the future, which is abruptly ended as Willy berates Linda for interrupting him in his violent enthusiasm for the boys' plans. Biff rises to his mother's defense: "Don't yell at her, Pop, will ya?" Willy, angered, replies, "What're you, takin' over this house?" Biff is furious. "Stop yelling at her." Willy leaves "beaten down, guilt ridden." The cause of the hatred between them is still unrevealed, but the fact of its existence is made unmistakably evident. . . .

The climactic scene of the series, the scene that reveals the cause of the separation of Biff and Willy, comes unex-pectedly in a restaurant washroom, where Willy relives the Boston hotel scene in which Biff finds him with a woman to whom he gives silk stockings. Biff in bitter tears exclaims, "You—you gave her Mama's stockings! . . . You fake! You phony little fake!" and runs out. Willy is kneeling on the washroom floor, pounding with his fists and yelling to Biff to come back, when a waiter enters and Willy realizes where he is. The remembered scene is hardly more sordid than the present one, for Willy's two sons have gone off with two common women, and left the sick man alone in the washroom with no thought for his welfare. Willy's lonesomeness has reached its peak. With dramatic acumen Arthur Miller has imposed the remembered scene, in which father and son are split apart, upon the action of the play, so that one incident reinforces the other, and Willy, although Biff has left with an appeal to Happy to save his father, is deserted by his son in this scene, as in the first. . . .

WILLY'S MISSED OPPORTUNITIES

Separating Willy and Biff is an irreparable loneliness, which is made all the more poignant by a momentary revelation of the love which could have been between them. Crying in his father's arms at the sordid failure of his life, Biff moves Willy to wonder and amazement that his son loves him; but Biff has already gone upstairs with the words, "I'll go in the morning," before Willy makes his discovery, "That boy— that boy is going to be magnificent!" Willy is immediately dreaming of Biff's success as a high school football star— "There's all kinds of important people in the stands," just before he drives off to kill himself.

In experiencing a "suffering self-recognition of separateness," Willy exemplifies the individual whose only aim is that kind of success which will gain him social approbation. The playwright, while highlighting the separation of Willy and Biff through a series of emotionally charged incidents, has packed the play with supporting scenes which, in other ways and through other characters, reflect and reiterate the lonesomeness of a character with Willy's lack of understanding. He could have been a good craftsman; he could have belonged by seeing around him his own creations. He could build a porch; he could plaster a ceiling; but a misguided idea of success led him to salesmanship with the mistaken thought that there was "comradeship" in it. Instead there was in it for Willy only biting lonesomeness.

WILLY'S SEPARATION FROM OTHERS

The other characters, through whom the theme is emphasized, appear and disappear as Willy's mind switches back and forth from present to past. The play opens and closes with the music of the flute, thin and poignant, representing the unknown musical father, for whose guidance Willy longs, and whose presence he cannot remember. Uncle Ben, the epitome of false standards of conduct, appears momentarily several times to misguide Willy and to isolate him further from the ideals to which he might have belonged. Charley and Bernard are a contrasting father and son to Willy and Biff. Through ideals of honesty and progress through hard work, Bernard attains the standing of a highly respected lawyer, to whom Charley points with modest pride, and at whom Willy can only shake his head and marvel. The contrast between Bernard and Biff is devastating even to Willy's dream of his son's success. The young boss, Howard, who fires Willy, completes Willy's separation from his work, and isolates him economically, as the others have psychologically. Howard's role is really only the technical fulfillment of the deterioration of Willy as a salesman, and is actually of minor importance.

Happy and Linda, the most important characters next to Willy and Biff, are unattached like them at the beginning and at the end, but in the flashbacks they appear as part of the unified family, reveling in the prospects of future attainments of the hero-sons. It is said of Linda in the stage directions that behind Willy's violence and his need for her she has always sensed in him

> a hovering presence which for thirty-five years she has never been able to predict or understand and which she has come to fear with a fear so deep that a moment ago, in the depths of her sleep, . . . she knew this presence had returned.

And in the end, in spite of the relief which it might seem she would feel after living so long "from day to day," she is really desolated by his death. Although her ideals were always higher than Willy's—for example, she detested the action of Uncle Ben in tripping up Biff—she never wished to impose them upon her husband. She followed where he led, even encouraging his dreams of success, although she recognized what Willy did not—that the facts did not support the dream. "She had developed an iron mastery of her objections to her husband," according to the playwright, and her encouragement of his idea of himself as an important salesman led only to an essential separation between them. Her reiteration, "Willy, darling, you're the handsomest man in the world," only brings to his mind a woman in a hotel room, as does her mending her stocking recall his gift of stockings to the woman. There is no companionable discussion between them, but only a boosting of Willy's ego by his wife who fears him, yet longs to please him.

Happy, likewise, adds emphasis to the theme of the loneliness of Willy, for Happy is a rubber stamp of Willy. He has not, like Biff, "ruined his life for spite," but he lives in the dream of being a much more important man than he is. Without aim in life or high standards of conduct, he lives on the pleasures of women and drink, and at Willy's funeral his philosophy is still

> He [Willy] had a good dream. It's the only dream you can have—to come out number-one man. He fought it out here, and this is where I'm gonna win it for him.

Misguided, lonesome—"My own apartment, a car, and plenty of women. And still, goddammit, I'm lonely"—Happy will never be different from his father. In him are seen the results of Willy's teaching personified in a second Willy. Whereas Biff in a sense revolted against his father's materialism, and deliberately became a failure, Happy is not even aware of the faults of his father's ideas and lives by them himself.

Thus Biff is alienated from Happy, who still lives in a dream of the future, and the two boys are alienated from Linda, who berates them for their lack of respect for Willy.

> There's no leeway any more. Either he's your father and you pay him that respect, or else you're not to come here.

And Linda is alienated from Willy because she knows no way to get along except to give in to him. When Bernard warns that if Biff doesn't buckle down, the football hero will flunk math, Linda says, "He's right, Willy, you've gotta—" whereupon Willy explodes in anger at her, "You want him to be a worm like Bernard? He's got spirit, personality . . ." and Linda, almost in tears, leaves the room. And, of course, the alienation of Willy and Biff plays the central part in the plot. The relationship of Willy and Happy, while not so clearly defined, obviously indicates a lack of friendship, for Willy feels he cannot turn to Happy for help when he loses his job, and says to Charley, who gives him money, "You're the only friend I got."

Thus each member of the family feels an isolation from the others, and thus the play is logically constructed so that the memories which appear upon the stage are those which come to Willy's mind as a result of the impact of his unhappiness. The lonesomeness of the hero is emphasized by this technique, for to him alone come the thoughts which are dramatized in incidents explaining the situation in which he finds himself. All the other characters of the play take part as he wills. The action, however, follows no casual plan in its forward movement. The careful design of the play is illustrated, for one example, by the build-up of suspense in the Willy-Biff series; but the theme of loneliness is emphasized by the fact that in essence the scenes are played by Willy alone with his dreams.

The Father/Son Relationship in *Death of a Salesman*

C.W.E. Bigsby

C.W.E. Bigsby writes that *Death of a Salesman* revolves around the relationship of Willy and his elder son Biff. In order to survive, Biff must break away from Willy by rejecting his father's values and ideals. Both men have an underlying sense of guilt that stems from the tension of their strained relationship. Moreover, both have a spiritual need that is unfulfilled and unrecognized because of their inability to discover what is meaningful in their lives. Indeed, there is a great gap between what the two men desire and the reality of their lives. Bigsby concludes that the love between the members of the Loman family is not strong enough to move Willy away from his self-destructive dreams and illusions.

C.W.E. Bigsby is a professor of American literature at the University of East Anglia, Norwich, England. He is the editor of *Cultural Change in the United States Since World War II*, and the author of *A Critical Introduction to Twentieth-Century American Drama*, *David Mamet*, and *Approaches to Popular Culture*.

Death of a Salesman is built around the relationship between Willy and his son, Biff. In his notebook Miller wrote himself a memo: '*Discover*... The link between Biff's work views and his anti W[1] feelings ... How it happens that W's life is in Biff's hands—aside from Biff succeeding. There is W's guilt to Biff in re: The Woman ... There is Biff's disdain for W's character, his false aims, his fictions, and these Biff

1. Willy

cannot finally give up or alter.' Here, as elsewhere in Miller's work, the relationship between father and son is a crucial one because it focusses the question of inherited values and assumptions, it dramatises deferred hopes and ideals, it becomes a microcosm of the debate between the generations, of the shift from a world still rooted in a simpler rural past to one in which that past exists simply as myth. It highlights the contrast between youthful aspirations and subsequent compromises and frustrations. It presents the submerged psychological tension which complicates the clear line of social action and personal morality. The family, so much an icon of American mythology, becomes the appropriate prism through which to view that mythology. The son's identity depends on creating a boundary between himself and his father, on perceiving himself outside the axial lines which had defined the father's world.

Biff and Willy's relationship is bedevilled by guilt. Willy feels guilty because he feels responsible for Biff's failure. Having discovered Willy with a woman in a Boston hotel room, he had refused to retake a mathematics examination, thereby abandoning his chance of reaching university and his access to a better career. But Biff equally feels guilty because he recognises a responsibility which he cannot fulfil, the responsibility to redeem Willy's empty life. In a telling speech, included in the notebook but excluded from the published and performed versions, Biff outlines his feelings explicitly.

> Willy—see?—I love you Willy. I've met ten or twelve Willys and you're only one of them.—I don't care what you do. I don't care if you live or die. You think I'm mad at you because of the Woman, don't you. I am, but I'm madder because you bitched up my life, *because* I can't tear you out of my heart, because *I keep trying* to make good, *do something* for you, to *succeed for you.*

If Biff loves Willy he also plainly hates him. Like the other characters he is composed of contradictions. Indeed, in his notes, Miller saw the conflict in Biff between his hatred for Willy and his own desire for success in New York as crucial to an understanding of the play as he did 'the combination of guilt (of failure), hate, and love—all in conflict' that Willy hopes to resolve 'by "accomplishing" a 20,000 dollar death'. Indeed, the ironies of the play flow out of contradiction in *Death of a Salesman*, much as they do in another sense in Beckett's *Waiting for Godot*. Action is immediately aborted, assertions withdrawn, hopes negated. Thus Willy complains of Biff that 'the trouble is he's lazy', only to reverse himself a few seconds later. 'There's one thing about Biff—he's not lazy.' Happy asserts that money holds no interest for him and that he would be happy with a free life in the West, only to ask immediately, 'The only thing is—what can you make out there?' The response to Biff's 'Let's go' is the same as that proffered in *Waiting for Godot*. They do not move. And so Happy regards himself as an idealist while taking 100-dollar bribes, Biff as rejecting a material life while stealing from his employer. For Willy, constant contradiction is a linguistic reflection of the collapse of rational control, but, more fundamentally, for all the Loman men it is indicative of a basic contradiction between their aspirations and the reality of their lives, between their setting and the essence of their dreams. They are denied peace because the philosophy on which they have built their lives involves competition, a restless pursuit of success, a desire to register a material achievement which they can conceive only in financial terms because they have neither the language nor the capacity to assess its significance in any other way. Hence Biff, who tries to retrace the steps of his father into the past and the West, is unable to accept a simple sense of harmony with his surroundings as adequate to the definition of success which his father has instilled in him, though that harmony is precisely what his father longs to achieve. As Biff explains to his brother,

> This farm I work on, it's spring there now, see? And they've got about fifteen new colts. There's nothing more inspiring or—beautiful than the sight of a mare and a new colt. And it's cool there now, see? Texas is cool now and it's spring. And whenever spring comes to where I am, I suddenly get the feeling, my God, I'm not getting anywhere! What the hell am I doing, playing around with horses, twenty-eight dollars a week! I'm thirty-five years old, I oughta be makin' my fortune. That's when I come running home. And now, I got here, and I don't know what to do with myself.

And so the lyricism, which is a powerful and crucial dimension of the play, defers to materialism, to a pragmatism which disrupts an incipient harmony and opens up a gap between Biff and his setting which, once closed, would not only offer him a simpler relationship between himself and the natural world but also still the conflict between his sensibility and his actions. He is, however, held back not only by the surviving dream of material success, a dream which he might be able to abandon, but also by the guilt which he feels towards Willy. He continues to feel responsible to a man who has warped his life but to whom his fate is ineluctably joined. In Miller's earliest draft the point is even more explicit:

W: . . . What do you want to be?

B: I want just to settle down and be somebody! Just a guy working in a store, or digging earth, or anything...

W: Then do it, do it.

B: You won't let me do it.

W: Me? When did I control you?

B: You do control me. I've stood in the most beautiful scenery in the world and cried in misery. I've galloped elegant horses and suddenly wanted to kill myself because I was letting you down. I want you to let me go, you understand. I want you to stop dreaming big dreams about me, and expecting anything great of me. I'm manual labor, Pop; one way or the other I'm a tramp, that's all. Can you make your peace with that...? I ask one thing. I want to be happy.

W: To enjoy yourself is not ambition. A tramp has that. Ambition is *things*. A man must want *things, things*.

In the final version these perceptions no longer need to surface in language. Biff and Willy remain bewildered for most of the play, unable to analyse the pressures at work on them, unable in particular to confess to the guilt, the love and the hate that connect and divide them. Willy's concern with things, meanwhile, is evident in his fascination with his refrigerator and his car but, most significantly, in his acquiescence in his own reduction to inanimate article to be marketed on appearance and image.

BIFF MUST REJECT HIS FATHER

In his first stage direction Miller insists on Willy's 'massive dreams and little cruelties', but in truth the play is concerned with suggesting that the adjectives might be legitimately reversed. And Biff, like his father, is still trying to buy love. As Miller wrote of the scene in the restaurant in which Biff and Happy abandon their father, 'Biff left out of guilt, pity, an inability to offer himself to W.' He recognises that Willy's desire that he should succeed is, in part at least, evidence of his love and, as Miller reminded himself, Biff 'still wants that evidence of W's love. Still does not want to be abandoned by him.' However, it is a love which threatens to destroy him, since it expresses itself in a desire on Willy's part to bequeath his son the thing he values most of all—his dream. The drama of the play emerges from the fact that Biff now gradually recognises the necessity for this abandonment. Indeed he has returned home with an intention not that remote from that of Chris Keller[2] or Gregers Werle.[3] 'He has returned home', Miller insists in his notes, 'resolved to disillusion W forever, to set him upon a new path, and thus release himself from responsibility for W and what he knows is going to happen to him—or half fears will.' There is the same passion for truth which springs from guilt and self-interest as had characterised the protagonists of *All My Sons* and *The Wild Duck*. But now Miller seems to recognise the necessity for this break with illusion. For here, it is finally not truth which kills, as it had been in *All My Sons*; it is a continued commitment to illusion. Biff breaks free; Willy does not. In his own eyes his death accomplishes the success that had evaded him in life, and, more importantly, it finally purges him of the guilt that he has felt for what he takes to be his son's failure. Since Biff had abandoned his potential career after finding Willy with another woman, Willy had thereafter felt responsible for his son's failure. And this is the principal tension of the play. In order for Biff to survive he has to release himself from his father and the values which he promulgates; in order for Willy to survive he has to cling to Biff and the conviction that material success is still possible. Thus guilt becomes the principal mechanism of human relationships. As Miller notes, 'Biff's conflict is that to tell the truth would be to diminish himself in his own eyes. To admit his fault. His confusion, then, is not didactic, or restricted to Willy' elucidation of salvation, but towards a surgical break which, he knows in his heart, W could never accept. His motive, then, is to destroy W, free himself.' In the final version it is not so clear. He is intent to save Willy's life as well as his own. His motivation is less obvious, his concern for his father largely genuine. And yet, of course, in saving Willy he will be freeing himself, so that the self apparently lies behind all actions. . . .

Biff and Willy feel a profound if unfocused sense of dissatisfaction with their lives. Beneath the monotony of daily survival is a yearning spirit, a perception of some kind of

2. the son in *All My Sons*   3. the son in Henrik Ibsen's *The Wild Duck*

spiritual need which they can only express through material correlatives or through stuttering encomiums to beauty or belonging. One of the problems of the play, indeed, derives from the fact that their lack of success actually confuses spiritual with financial failure. The more significant question is whether material success would have blunted or indeed even satisfied that need and, though this might have brought Miller perilously close to cliché, his portrait of Bernard—moral, hard-working, successful, attractive—is perhaps in danger of validating the dreams which Willy had had for Biff. Willy had, admittedly, regarded such success as an inevitable product of life in America and had taught Biff to take what he could not earn, and yet in some way the adequacy of that success is not challenged in Bernard's case. Indeed he seems to represent the apparently untroubled serenity which is the reward of honest toil. Indeed, it was not until *After the Fall* that he chose to question the adequacy of that portrait, taking as his protagonist a lawyer whose success, like that of Bernard, is marked by his appealing a case before the Supreme Court. Then he was to query the value of success even when it is the product of effort and application. Uncle Ben might be a portrait of a Horatio Alger figure, stumbling over wealth, but Bernard is in many ways an idealised figure. The danger is that he is not only a model for Willy of what his sons might have become; he also becomes a model for Miller.

The dice are loaded against Willy. In the original notes he was literally to have been a little man. Miller chose to transform that into an obesity apparent in the text but ignored when Lee J. Cobb was cast for the central role: 'I'm fat. I'm very—foolish to look at, Linda . . . as I was going in to see the buyer I heard him say something about—walrus. And I—I cracked him right across the face.' Even allowing for the exaggeration of self-pity, this offers a clue to his failure as a salesman. His misfortune was that he chose a career in which appearance was everything, at a time and in a country in which appearance was primary. As Biff was to have said in an early draft, and as is apparent but not voiced in precisely these words in the final version, 'The pity of it is, that he was happy only on certain Sundays, with a warm sun on his back, and a trowel in his hand, some good wet cement, and something to build. That's who he really was.' As a salesman he has always to dissemble, to smile, to put up a front. He is an actor who has increasingly lost his audience. His life is a falsehood. But perhaps there is a certain naivety in the assumption, no less Miller's than that of one of his characters, Charley, that the situation is fundamentally different for others, for his contrast of the life of the salesman with that of a man who can 'tell you the law' seems to be justified by the character of Bernard. The real force of the play suggests otherwise. For Miller implies that Willy had the wrong dreams, not simply that his methods of fulfilling those dreams were wrong. With Eugene O'Neill he seems to suggest that Willy's mistake was to imagine that he could gain possession of his soul through gaining possession of the world. In that respect he was paradigmatic. Charley and Bernard are successful and humane, but they, too, live a life whose intimacies seem lacking. Where is the love between them? The problem is that the light is never swung in their direction and thus it is possible to see in them a vindication of the material success which they represent.

THE FAILURE OF LOVE IN THE LOMAN FAMILY

Biff's anger at his father derives partly from Willy's weakness and helplessness, partly from his bitterness, but partly also from his love for him, a love which won't cut Biff loose from his own sense of guilt. To absolve his father would be to admit to his own weakness and culpability. As Miller wrote in his notebook,

> Biff's conflict is that to tell the truth would be to diminish himself in his own eyes. To admit to his own fault. The truth is that though W did overbuild B's ego, and then betrayed him, Biff feels guilt in his vengeance on W knowing that he also is incompetent. Through this confession of his having *used* W's betrayal, W sees his basic love, and is resolved to suicide.

Again the final version of the play deflects this confession into action, intensifying the force by refraining from discharging its energy through words. Thus Biff, having denounced his father and admitted to his own inability to command more than a dollar an hour, breaks down in tears, 'holding on to Willy, who dumbly fumbles for Biff's face'. And love, which Miller has said was in a race for Willy's soul, becomes the very mechanism which pulls Willy towards his death.

Willy Loman and the American Dream

Harold Clurman

In his 1949 review of *Death of a Salesman*, Harold Clurman explains that the play challenges the American dream. He writes that there are really two American dreams: the historical dream that offers the promise of equality and opportunity, and the business success dream that is built on the idea that profit is an end in itself.

According to Clurman, Willy Loman has fallen under the spell of the success dream. Willy believes that being well liked and having money will solve life's problems and, ultimately, result in happiness. Willy's false dream torments the entire Loman household.

Harold Clurman was a professor of theater, stage director, and theater critic. His works include *On Directing, Ibsen,* and *The Divine Pastime: Theatre Essays.* He contributed essays on drama to *Esquire,* the *New York Times,* and *Partisan Review.*

Arthur Miller's *Death of a Salesman* is one of the outstanding plays in the repertory of the American theatre. That its theme is not, strictly speaking, new to our stage—Arthur Richman's *Ambush* (1921), J.P. McEvoy's *The Potters* (1923), Elmer Rice's *The Adding Machine* (1923), George Kelly's *The Show-Off* (1924), Clifford Odets' *Awake and Sing* and *Paradise Lost* (1935) being in this respect its antecedents—does not in any way lessen its effect or significance. The value of *Death of a Salesman* lies in the fact that it states its theme with penetrating clarity in our era of troubled complacency.

Death of a Salesman is a challenge to the American dream. Lest this be misunderstood, I hasten to add that there are two versions of the American dream. The historical

American dream is the promise of a land of freedom with opportunity and equality for all. This dream needs no challenge, only fulfillment. But since the Civil War, and particularly since 1900, the American dream has become distorted to the dream of business success. A distinction must be made even in this. The original premise of our dream of success—popularly represented in the original boy parables of Horatio Alger—was that enterprise, courage and hard work were the keys to success. Since the end of the First World War this too has changed. Instead of the ideals of hard work and courage, we have salesmanship. Salesmanship implies a certain element of fraud: the ability to put over or sell a commodity regardless of its intrinsic usefulness. The goal of salesmanship is to make a deal, to earn a profit—the accumulation of profit being an unquestioned end in itself.

THE PSYCHOLOGY OF THE SUCCESS DREAM

This creates a new psychology. To place all value in the mechanical act of selling and in self-enrichment impoverishes the human beings who are rendered secondary to the deal. To possess himself fully, a man must have an intimate connection with that with which he deals as well as with the person with whom he deals. When the connection is no more than an exchange of commodities, the man himself ceases to be a man, becomes a commodity himself, a spiritual cipher.

This is a humanly untenable situation. The salesman realizes this. Since his function precludes a normal human relationship, he substitutes an imitation of himself for the real man. He sells his "personality." This "personality," now become only a means to an end—namely, the consummated sale—is a mask worn so long that it soon comes to be mistaken, even by the man who wears it, as his real face. But it is only his commercial face with a commercial smile and a commercial aura of the well-liked, smoothly adjusted, oily cog in the machine of the sales apparatus.

This leads to a behavior pattern which is ultimately doomed; not necessarily because of the economic system of which it is the human concomitant, but quite simply because a man is not a machine. The death of Arthur Miller's salesman is symbolic of the breakdown of the whole concept of salesmanship inherent in our society.

Miller does not say these things explicitly. But it is the

strength of his play that it is based on this understanding, and that he is able to make his audience realize it no matter whether or not they are able consciously to formulate it. When the audience weeps at *Death of a Salesman*, it is not so much over the fate of Willy Loman—Miller's pathetic hero—but over the millions of such men who are our brothers, uncles, cousins, neighbors. The lovable lower-middle-class mole Willy Loman represents is related to a type of living and thinking in which nearly all of us—"professionals" as well as salesmen—share.

ARTHUR MILLER MEETS A SALESMAN

In his book Broadway Anecdotes, *Peter Hay relates the story of Arthur Miller's encounter with an old high school friend who worked as a salesman.*

Playwright Arthur Miller was once sitting in a bar, when a well-dressed and slightly tipsy man came up to him:

"Aren't you Arthur Miller?"

"Yes, I am."

"Don't you remember me?"

Miller couldn't quite place him.

"Art, it's me—Sam! I'm your old buddy from high school. We used to go out on double dates!"

Sam went on, filling Miller in on all that happened to him since those days and how well he had done working as a salesman at a department store. Finally he stopped and asked:

"And what do you do, Art?"

"Well, I write . . ."

"What, Art?"

"Plays mainly."

"Any of them produced?"

"Yeah . . ."

"Would I know any of them?"

"Perhaps you've heard of *Death of a Salesman*?"

Sam was finally speechless. He turned white as it sank in, and then he cried:

"Why, you're Arthur Miller!"

Willy Loman never acknowledges or learns the error of his way. To the very end he is a devout believer in the ideology that destroys him. He believes that life's problems are all solved by making oneself "well liked" (in the salesman's sense) and by a little cash. His wife knows only that he is a good man and that she must continue to love him. His sons, who are his victims, as he has been of the false dream by which he has lived, draw different conclusions from his failure. The younger boy, Hap, believes only that his father was an incompetent (as do many of the play's commentators), but he does not reject his father's ideal. (It is to be noted that in a very important sense Willy Loman is sympathetic precisely because of his failure to make himself a successful machine.) The older boy, Biff, comes to understand the falsity of his father's ideal and determines to set out on a new path guided by a recovery of his true self.

There are minor flaws in *Death of a Salesman*, such as the constant pointing to a secret in the older brother's past which is presumed to be the immediate cause of his moral breakdown—the secret turning out to be the boy's discovery of his father's marital infidelity. There is validity in this scene as part of the over-all picture of the father-son relationship. A shock such as the boy sustains here often serves to propel people into the unexplored territory of their subconscious, and may thus become the springboard for further and more basic questioning. Miller's error here is to make the boy's horror at his father's "deceit" appear crucial rather than contributory to the play's main line.

Some people have objected that the use of the stream-of-consciousness technique—the play dramatizes Willy's recollection of the past, and at times switches from a literal presentation of his memory to imaginary and semisymbolic representation of his thought—is confusing, and a sign of weakness in the author's grasp of his material.

These objections do not impress me. The limitations of *Death of a Salesman* are part of its virtues. The merit in Miller's treatment of his material lies in a certain clean, moralistic rationalism. It is not easy to make the rational a poetic attribute, but Miller's growth since *All My Sons* consists in his ability to make his moral and rationalistic characteristics produce a kind of poetry.

The truth of *Death of a Salesman* is conveyed with what might be compared to a Living Newspaper, documentary accuracy. With this there is a grave probity and a sensitivity that raise the whole beyond the level of what might otherwise have seemed to be only agitation and propaganda. Other playwrights may be more colorful, lyrical and rich with the fleshed nerves and substance of life; Miller holds us with a sense of his soundness. His play has an ascetic, slate-like hue, as if he were eschewing all exaggeration and extravagance; and with a sobriety that is not without humor, yet entirely free of frivolity, he issues the forthright commandment, "Thou shalt not be a damn' fool!"

Elia Kazan's production is first rate. It is true to Miller's qualities, and adds to them a swift directness, muscularity and vehemence of conviction. If any further criticism is in order I should say the production might have gained a supplementary dimension if it had more of the aroma of individual characterization, more intimacy, more of the quiet music of specific humanity—small, as the people in the play are small, and yet suggestive of those larger truths their lives signify.

CHAPTER 4

The Crucible

READINGS ON
ARTHUR MILLER

The Historical Background of *The Crucible*

Henry Popkin

Henry Popkin compares the communist scare of the 1950s with the Salem witch trial that is the basis for *The Crucible*. Popkin then rates both events as source material for serious drama. He suggests that the Salem trial is a difficult topic for tragedy because the witchcraft charges are unreasonable and heaped upon individuals who are entirely blameless. Hence, Popkin suggests that it was imperative that Miller construct a more concrete source of guilt—adultery—for the main character, John Proctor.

Henry Popkin contributes theater reviews for the *London Times* and *Vogue*. He writes extensively about modern American and European drama.

Although *The Crucible* is set in seventeenth-century America, Arthur Miller intended it as a comment on American life of his own time. For several years before the play opened in 1953, public investigations had been examining and interrogating radicals, former radicals, and possible former radicals, requiring witnesses to tell about others and not only about themselves. The House Committee to Investigate Un-American Activities evolved a memorable and much-quoted sentence: "Are you now, or have you ever been a member of the Communist Party?" Borrowing a phrase from a popular radio program, its interrogators called it "the $64 question."

THE INFLUENCE OF JOSEPH MCCARTHY

Senator Joseph McCarthy built his international fame on his presumed knowledge of subversion in government and added a new word to our vocabulary—"McCarthyism," meaning ruinous accusation without any basis in evidence.

From "Arthur Miller's *The Crucible*" by Henry Popkin, *College English*, vol. 26, no. 2, November 1964, pp. 139–46. Reprinted courtesy of the National Council of Teachers of English.

A few months before *The Crucible* reached Broadway, McCarthy had helped to elect a President of the United States, and, two days before the premiere, that President was inaugurated. The elections had made McCarthy chairman of an important congressional subcommittee; his power was greater than ever. The film and television industries gave every sign of being terrified by McCarthyism—but by the atmosphere that McCarthy created, more than by his own subcommittee. Show business found itself of more interest to the House Committee to Investigate Un-American Activities than to Senator McCarthy's subcommittee. Blacklists barred certain actors and writers from working in the popular media. Actors who refused to give testimony disappeared both from the large film screen and the small television screen, but "friendly witnesses" continued to work. On the other hand, the New York stage, since it was and still is a relatively chaotic enterprise, was comparatively unmanaged and untouched. Nevertheless, *The Crucible* was a bold as well as a timely play, written at a time when the congressional investigators had the power to do considerable damage. Senator McCarthy's personal authority wilted in the following year, but Miller was a somewhat unfriendly witness before a congressional committee in 1956. He described his own flirtation with Communism but refused to give the names of Communists he had known. He was ultimately absolved of the charge of contempt of the committee.

HISTORICAL PARALLELS IN *THE CRUCIBLE*

The Crucible dramatized the phrase that was popularly being used to describe the congressional hearings—"witch hunts." In the Salem witch trials, Miller chose an unmistakable parallel to current events. He has never permitted any doubt that the parallel was deliberate. In his introduction to his *Collected Plays* and in his interpretative remarks scattered through the text, he calls attention to the play's contemporary reference and invites comparisons between the two widely separated hearings.

The Salem witch trials are, equally, a historical event. In 1692, in Salem, Massachusetts, twenty people were found guilty of witchcraft and hanged; others who had been accused saved themselves by confessing to witchcraft and accusing others. As in the unhappy occurrences of the 1950's, naming others was taken to be a guarantee of sincerity and of a laudable desire to tell all. Also, the witchcraft scare was violent, alarming, and brief, like an epidemic and, again, like the Communist scare of the 1950's. It will be easy enough to discover and to expound still other parallels as we examine the play, but one preliminary difficulty needs to be stated: the parallel fails at one important point. There is such a thing as Communism; there is no such thing as witchcraft. This distinction indicates that the psychological state of the victims of the Salem trials is somewhat different from that of the victims of the investigations of the 1950's. Of course, people suffered equally in both centuries, and, while it may seem callous to weigh one anguish against another and to say that one man's suffering means more than another's, it is necessary to observe that the situation of our own time is more complex and therefore potentially more useful to the artist.

THE SALEM WITCH TRIALS AS A SOURCE OF DRAMA

The distinction I am making is the same one that Aristotle made in our first treatise on literature, the *Poetics*. Aristotle writes that we are appalled by the suffering of the entirely blameless; such suffering, says Aristotle, is too disturbing to be a suitable subject for tragedy. Instead, we expect our tragic characters to exhibit some weakness, some sort of flaw. Scholars have disagreed for centuries as to the kind of flaw that Aristotle meant, but it is safe to say that the tragic hero is somehow imperfect and that his imperfection has some connection with his tragic catastrophe.

The unfortunate condemned innocents of Salem did nothing to bring on their ruin, nothing, at least, that had anything to do with the charge against them. Let me qualify that statement: it is conceivable that one aged eccentric or another actually thought she was in communication with the devil. That delusion is too special—not to say too lunatic—to be a very likely, interesting, or useful state of mind for a serious character. Miller seems to be of this opinion, since the only person in *The Crucible* who believes herself to be a witch is Tituba, who is not fully developed as a character and remains a minor figure. Furthermore, she confesses and is not executed; she need not suffer any pangs of conscience over her presumed witchcraft. If she thinks she has been a witch, she must also think she has atoned by confessing. The others, the true martyrs of Salem, had the consolation of knowing that they were innocent. Certainly, they were heroic in maintaining their innocence at a time when false confession was likely to save their lives. But to be heroic is not necessarily to be the complex, dramatic character who gives life to drama.

THE COMMUNIST SCARE AS A SOURCE OF DRAMA

The events of the 1950's provided a more logical connection between character and fate. The American Communist Party existed, and, for a long time, its legality was unquestioned. It was perfectly possible and legal to join it—for any of a variety of reasons, both good and bad—for idealistic reasons, out of a desire for power, out of an instinctive interest in conspiracy, out of a general dissatisfaction with society, or even, as many later said, in order to offer effective opposition to Fascism. It was possible for many, like Miller himself, to have some association with Communism and Communists without joining the party. Great numbers of those accused in the 1950's came from the ranks of these party members and their non-member "fellow traveller" associates. Still others among the accused had no connection with the Communist Party; for the purposes of our comparison, they are exactly like the innocent victims of the Salem trials.

I have set up these elementary categories in order to demonstrate that the actor or director who was blacklisted and so lost his job in the 1950's was likely to have made some commitment in the 1930's that affected his subsequent fate. This was not necessarily so, but it was likely. He had not made a commitment to Satan, and few will now say that such a man deserved to be banished from his profession because of his past or present politics, but, in his case, we can say that character and fate roughly, very roughly, fit together, that there is a meaningful connection between what the man did and what later happened to him. Life is not always so logical, as the Salem trials tell us. The witchcraft trials in Salem were wild, unreasonable offenses against justice; they present intrinsic difficulties for any dramatist who wants to make an orderly drama out of them. Art tends to be neater and, superficially, more logical than the history of Salem. In contrast, the corresponding events of the 1950's have a cruel and inaccurate logic; their injustice is, in a sense, logical, even though the logic is reprehensible.

JOHN PROCTOR'S GUILT

If we were not able to point out that the historical parallel in *The Crucible* is imperfect, we might still justifiably object that the impact of a sudden and undeserved punishment upon entirely innocent people is a difficult subject for drama. Aristotle's criticism of the entirely blameless hero continues to be valid. In apparent recognition of this principle, Miller has constructed a new sort of guilt for his hero, John Proctor. In the play, Proctor has been unfaithful to his wife, and Miller goes out of his way to assure us directly that his infidelity violates his personal code of behavior. The girl whom he loved, jealous and resentful of being rejected, accuses Proctor's wife of witchcraft, and so Proctor, who has, in this peculiar fashion, caused his wife to be accused, has a special obligation to save her. In trying to save her, he is himself charged with witchcraft. So, he does suffer for his guilt—but for a different guilt, for adultery, not for witchcraft.

Character Profiles in *The Crucible*

Bernard F. Dukore

Each of the major characters in *The Crucible* faces a test of integrity—each enters a personal crucible. As the play unfolds, the audience observes how the characters respond when their motives, beliefs, and fears conflict with the hysteria found in Salem. Bernard F. Dukore lists the main players and assesses their integrity when their ethics, reputation, and instinct for self-preservation are at stake.

Bernard F. Dukore is a professor of theater arts and humanities at Virginia Polytechnic Institute in Blacksburg. He has written extensively about the theater, playwrights, and dramatic theory and criticism.

JOHN PROCTOR

Despite the impression that Proctor is sceptical enough to perceive from the start the truth behind the crying-out of witchcraft, the fact is that once he and Abigail are alone, she dismisses the notion of witchcraft as tosh and confides to him part of the truth about Betty Parris's illness. He is not as good as Rebecca, he wavers before committing himself to a course of action, and he is sufficiently unvirtuous to have had an affair with a teenager. He is physically but not morally strong (if the '*strikingly beautiful*' Abigail's behaviour in the play is an indication, she may have been the one to take the initiative). Although he does not like the smell of authority, in his phrase, the odour bothers him only when others exert it over him: he does not hesitate to use it upon his servant, to whom he brandishes a whip. As Miller says, Proctor is not only a sinner against the morality of his time, he sins against his own view of decency. Instead of a virtuous man exercising his virtue, he is a troubled soul who discovers, to his surprise, that he has virtue. He rejects the ad-

From Death of a Salesman *and* The Crucible: *Text and Performance* by Bernard F. Dukore (Atlantic Highlands, NJ: Humanities Press, 1989). Copyright ©1989 by Bernard F. Dukore. Reprinted with permission of Macmillan Press Ltd.

vances of Abigail, who would rekindle his ardour, but he is less than open with his wife, to whom he lies about Abigail (they had been alone together) and about Elizabeth's cooking (he added salt to the food: their marriage lacks this and other spices). Unlike Willy Loman, he evaluates himself justly. His guilt of adultery links to his innocence of witchcraft. He recognises that despite his sinfulness his nature makes him refuse to commit an unjust act (to agree to the posting of his signed confession would make him an exemplar of a lie and, as the play reiterates, God damns all liars). Thus, he can die with honour and goodness, albeit only a shred, which suffices to give him self-respect.

REVEREND JOHN HALE

Unlike Proctor, Reverend Hale ends with less stature than he begins. While he expresses misgivings about the trials to the Proctors, he believes the Devil is a real enemy. Though suspicious that the condemned confess to avoid being hanged, he tries to maintain his faith in the court, for the Church is the foundation of his life. With Elizabeth's arrest and Mary's hearing, his doubts about the reliability of the witnesses accumulate until he concludes that Proctor, not Abigail, is truthful. After he denounces the court, he subverts his clerical office by counselling the condemned to lie, for he hopes God damns liars less than those who throw away His most precious gift, life, for pride. Elizabeth calls his reasoning diabolical. Ironically, his belief that to die for nothing does no good is close to today's common viewpoint.

GILES COREY

Like Proctor, Corey goes to his death heroically. Unlike Proctor, he is not hanged. Since he would be hanged and his property auctioned if he responded to the charges, he neither confirms nor denies them. When the authorities lay large stones upon his chest, his only words are 'More weight'. Whereas Proctor dies for a principle, his righteous name, Corey dies as he lives, for property: as silence would qualify him for Christian burial, his property would go to his sons.

REBECCA NURSE

Like Proctor a force that represents the good, Rebecca also resembles him in a modern outlook. His transgression and guilt draw sympathy from contemporary audiences. Her understanding of children is more closely allied to our time than to hers. Dismissing the notion that they are bewitched by the Devil, this mother of eleven observes that the 'silly seasons' of youngsters enable them to 'run the Devil bow-legged' and that patience will enable one to catch a child's spirit, which through love will return of its own accord. When she hears that Hale might try to exorcise the Demon from Betty Parris's body, this godly woman's only concern is that the child might be hurt. When in the last act Proctor confesses to witchcraft, she hopes God will show mercy to him for having lied. Since to lie would be to damn her soul, she refuses to confess. Miller does not overemphasise her goodness but establishes her as a rebuke to the madness of others and a goal towards which Proctor may aspire.

MILLER'S VIEW OF THE INDIVIDUAL IN SOCIETY

In his plays, Arthur Miller establishes a tension-filled relationship between society and the individual. In a conversation with psychologist Richard Evans, from the book Psychology and Arthur Miller, *the playwright states that* The Crucible *illustrates this tension from the perspective of individual characters as they interact in society;* Death of a Salesman, *on the other hand, illustrates this tension as a struggle within the individual.*

MILLER: *The Crucible* is involved essentially with the social relations of human beings, and consequently, the predominant emphasis in writing the play was on the conflict between people rather than the conflict within somebody. In *Death of a Salesman*, the emphasis is more subjective, principally, I suppose, because what I was interested in there was what Willy's world and his life had done to his personality and how he was struggling with the total experience that he had lived through. As a matter of fact, the title that I started with was *The Inside of His Head*, and at one time I thought of having a vast proscenium with a face that opened and the whole play taking place inside his skull. It's a matter of emphasis; you can do certain things better with one approach than you can with another. *The Crucible* is in a more epic form; the individual is seen through society. The other is in a more realistic or psychological form; society is seen through the individual.

ELIZABETH PROCTOR

Sensitive enough to feel sad to have killed a rabbit, who had wandered into the house, for supper, Elizabeth is initially cold, unforgiving and uncharitable towards her formerly unfaithful husband. Rightly, critics have made much of the crucial scene of Act III wherein to save her husband's reputation she lies about his adultery. What requires notice is that in doing so she contrasts with Abigail, for Elizabeth lies to *save* another's life, and that in Act IV, she confesses guilt—an *honest* confession, in contrast to the one Danforth tempts Proctor to make, which helps to solder the private and public areas of the play. Recognising her own sins, she admits that a cold wife is required to provoke adultery. Whereas she fails to forgive him in Act II, she begs him to forgive her in Act IV. Like Linda Loman, she has the last words in the play. Her final speech, proclaiming Proctor's goodness, brings a note of triumph to his death.

ABIGAIL WILLIAMS

Partly a malign parody of the seduced and abandoned orphan, Abigail is a passionate young woman with unsatiated sexual needs. She condemns Elizabeth for coldness. A forceful personality, Abigail is able to bend the other girls to her will and intelligent enough to convince the pillars of society of her truthfulness. At a polar extreme from Rebecca Nurse, she is the most evil person in the play, who would kill to gain the man for whom she lusts. Initially impelled by the twin motives of lust for Proctor and desire for self-preservation, both motives turn to lust for power.

DEPUTY GOVERNOR, JUDGE DANFORTH

Since Judge Danforth is convinced of his cause's justice and his own probity, he takes an assault on the court to be an attack on himself. He is sufficiently honest that he wavers when it appears that Mary may be telling the truth, but he wonders whether Proctor may unconsciously desire to undermine the court, for he himself has seen people choked by spirits. It makes sense to summon Elizabeth to verify her husband's admission of adultery with Abigail, who denies the charge. When in the final act Danforth tries to exact a confession from Proctor, he insists that it is not a lie to save his life. However blinded he may be, Danforth's religious convictions are sincere (though no less insidious than Abigail's actions).

Reverend Samuel Parris

A weak, mean-spirited man, Parris believes himself to be persecuted by enemies, and since he sincerely tries to win them to godliness, he cannot understand why people resist him. Though a minister, his chief concern is less God than his authority. If his daughter trafficked with spirits in the heathen forest, then his enemies may use her action to ruin him. Deferential towards the powerful, he is a petty tyrant to the helpless Black slave Tituba, at whom he screams as soon as she enters the room. Terrified that his home may be associated with diabolical influences, he is relieved when Hale suggests that if this be the case it is because the Devil wants to subvert the best. Only apparently does he reverse himself in Act IV. Then as before, he aims to save himself, for the populace, now opposed to the witch-hunters, has threatened him. But he is not a cardboard villain. His suspicion that the girls conjured evil spirits proves justified. Although Proctor scores off him comically for his demand that he have the deed to his house, he is Salem's third preacher in seven years and fears being 'put out like the cat whenever some majority feels the whim'.

Tituba

A reminder of rigid class divisions in Salem (Proctor behaves towards Mary much as Parris does towards Tituba), the Barbados slave also parallels Abigail. When Parris threatens Tituba with whipping and Putnam threatens her with hanging, she acts upon Abigail's example. She pleads that she was an unwilling accomplice of the Devil and that someone else bewitched the girls. Unable to imagine whom to identify as witches, she is wily enough to verify names suggested by others.

Proctor, the Moral Hero in *The Crucible*

Sidney Howard White

In his plays, Arthur Miller works to clarify moral issues. According to Sidney Howard White, John Proctor, the hero of *The Crucible*, faces the injustices of society in a manner reminiscent of the heroes in the plays of Norwegian playwright Henrik Ibsen. Proctor is a simple man whose moral conscience is tested by the hysteria in Salem. At the end of the play, Proctor affirms his moral honesty and integrity by refusing to reveal publicly his confession of guilt. In short, he emerges as a strong human being who maintains his good name.

Sidney Howard White is a professor of English at the University of Rhode Island. He has published books on *The Scarlet Letter*, *The Great Gatsby*, and Arthur Miller.

Essential in Miller's view of tragedy is the clarification of some lesson, "the discovery of the moral law." This, of course, is what has always made Miller unique in comparison to most modern playwrights who, if anything, profess only the certainty of moral *un*certainty. Miller's tragic figure is compelled to act, to evaluate himself as a man according to certain very definite convictions. And in losing the battle, his "attempt posits a wrong or an evil in his environment." This, according to Miller, is "precisely the morality of tragedy and its lesson." What is of particular interest to us here, in Miller's re-definition of the classical tragic lesson, is how well it fits the predicament of the man of determined action in modern life. The weight of the drama, appropriately enough, falls on the injustices and limitations inherent in today's social systems.

Miller has been moralizing in a major way ever since *All*

My Sons. The appearance of the *The Crucible* in 1953 is a kind of high-water mark of Miller's ability to moralize with great effectiveness. In this sense, Miller's adaptation of Henrik Ibsen's *An Enemy of the People* in 1950 is within what could be called a preparatory line of development. In Ibsen's play we have the man of necessary action again, Dr. Stockmann, who cannot stand by while a social injustice seems about to be committed. Even though it will bring his ruin, he must act according to his convictions and be the battler against the forces of evil and gross materialism. The "line of development" to *The Crucible* through Ibsen is, therefore, a very natural one for Miller. John Proctor in Miller's play follows what he believes is a moral line of conduct, and in dying for it, posits the lesson involved—in this case, the right to personal integrity.

What should be noted quickly, however, is the way these "lessons for life" become apparent in Miller's plays. In keeping with his often restated view that the tragic lesson—or, simply, "the truth"—is primary, notice how the other conditions have intended secondary roles. According to Miller's theory, Joe Keller's theatrically effective defense of his immoral conduct (*All My Sons*) is actually secondary to the lesson we learn in seeing him die for it. His dream was false; he suffers for it; we—if Miller's theory be correct—gain by the lesson. Nearly all critics agree, however, that the effect is accomplished in rather crude, melodramatic ways. Or simply, the dramatic theory is bigger than the play, and seems outwardly contrived.

In the same sense, the "discovery" of truth in *Death of a Salesman* must also be within a reverse set of circumstances, in which the pursuit of false dreams must point to the reverse for the audience—the clear demarcation of the right dreams. This specific task, the pointing to the right dream, is given to Biff Loman. Miller later admitted that he was disappointed in the critics' general neglect of such intentions. Biff was meant to represent "the system of love," and Willy's belated recognition that his son loved him was meant as a contrast to Willy's "law of success." Moralizing, as such, becomes far simpler and more direct in *Enemy of the People* and *The Crucible.* Both chief characters have the immediate advantage of being on the side of "the right" from the very opening of the action. There is no need, therefore, to be continually seeing the truth, or the lesson, by refraction, as it were, in a mirror of evil deeds. All lessons are gained simply by watching the continuing action of the play and being affected by the increasingly crucial nature of their ordeals.

PROCTOR'S MORAL STRENGTH IS TESTED

What we now have in *The Crucible* is Miller's first clearly recognized heroic man. Consistent with Miller's views of contemporary twentieth-century life, *The Crucible* is a believable, careful parallel of modern issues. *The* obvious issue for the early 1950's was the investigation of Communist subversion in the country headed by Senator Joseph McCarthy. Miller admits the relation of the McCarthy "witch hunts" to his own subject, the notorious witch hunts of old Salem in 1692. Miller's motivations for speaking out in such a deliberate manner in 1953 are consistent with what might be called his growing social belligerency in the face of certain causes. Here, as Miller has pointed out, the cause is actually mass hysteria. His aim is to "show that the sin of public terror . . . divests man of conscience." The analogy to current events would be self-evident.

Miller used the actual accounts of the Salem witch trials as the basis for his play. Nearly all the major characters were taken from real life. His task, as a dramatist, was to focus on the issue of mass hysteria, and to draw out of such involvements a believable context for certain heroic and necessary acts. In essence, then, John Proctor is true to his portrait in history; "there is evidence to suggest," Miller says of Proctor, "that he had a sharp and biting way with hypocrites." The issue for Proctor as a man becomes more and more central as the play develops. The plot moves quickly, aided by the machinations of the servant girl, Abigail, from the issue of his wife being accused of witchcraft to the issue of himself being accused. Early in the play the love-vengeance triangle has been established between the three, and remains as a kind of hidden presence to be brought out on cue whenever the turns in the plot—or even outright theatricality—demand it. Although the main thrust of the play is along the lines of the public hysteria, essential reality is served by our quick acceptance of Abigail's attachment for Proctor. What raises Proctor higher and higher in our estimation is his sincere feeling of uneasiness in being forced to play the hero's role. Appropriate to the Puritan Code, he feels himself a sinner through his actual involvement with Abigail.

One of the most theatrically effective scenes is the one

where Proctor admits to his carnal sin before the court in order to discredit Abigail in her attack against his wife, Elizabeth. The admission, which at first seems to be a successful ploy, turns completely against him when Elizabeth is trapped into lying about her real knowledge of their affair. His stature as Miller's man of conscience is finally tested and assured in his decision at the end of the play to give his life rather than confess to the crime of witchcraft. Miller leaves us with the impression that the act broke "the power of theocracy in Massachusetts."

PROCTOR AFFIRMS HIS MORAL HONESTY

The manner in which the plot shifts and then hinges on his ability to affirm his moral honesty provides another question in our assessment of Miller's theory and practice as a playwright. Here again, as in the previous plays, the effective end-result of the play somewhat overrides the previous action. We are meant to believe, in the last act, that the saving of the town (and the end of theocracy in the state) will now depend entirely on Proctor's sacrifice. Somewhat weakly at the beginning of this last act we are given the facts of possible dissolution which are meant to alter radically all the previous conditions which have held us up to that point. The foremost alteration is the abrupt absence of the adversary, Abigail (and the fanaticism she represents), from Salem and the play. The condition which is meant to have our complete concentration, now that the screams and terrorizing of the girls is over, seems too pristine clear and unsullied compared to the nightmarish echoes of the recent witch-crying. We are now asked simply to see if Proctor can lose himself and save the town.

His dilemma now must come down to what he is willing to do to remain a proper human. Miller gives us a few dramatic shifts—or vacillations—in the possibilities open to Proctor. Minutes before the dawn, the dawn of his hanging, he consents to confess ("I cannot mount the gibbet like a saint"). At first, the confession almost fails because of his unwillingness to implicate others. Next, he signs but will not surrender the paper to Judge Danforth to be used publicly. "Is there no good penitence but it be public?" Finally, what must be the real issue to Proctor—what bars him from the false confession—breaks through: he will not give his name. "How may I live without my name? I have given you my soul; leave me my name!"

Profiles of Elizabeth Proctor and Abigail Williams in *The Crucible*

C.J. Partridge

C.J. Partridge explores the psychological makeup of the fictionalized characters Abigail Williams and Elizabeth Proctor in *The Crucible*. He finds Abigail to be a complex individual who possesses insight into human nature, a powerful strength of will, and driving passion. John Proctor's rejection of Abigail transforms these characteristics into a destructive force that spreads into the community in the form of hysteria. Elizabeth, caught in a strained relationship with her husband, is defined by two character weaknesses, suspicion and coldness. Partridge argues that at the end of the play, ironically at the time of John's death, Elizabeth acknowledges her weaknesses and subsequently achieves greater self-knowledge.

C.J. Partridge is an assistant professor in the Department of English at the University of Victoria, B.C., Canada. His writings include *Minor American Fiction, 1920–1940: A Survey and an Introduction, Death of a Salesman (A. Miller)*, and *Coriolanus (Shakespeare)*.

At first it may seem that Abigail Williams is primarily responsible for the climate of hysteria in Salem. But, as with so many situations in real life, the more one considers the origin of a phenomenon the more difficult it becomes to assign guilt and responsibility. One may try always to endorse the aphorism 'To understand all is to forgive all.' Is there anything that can be forgiven in so obviously malicious a character as Abigail?

THE DECEITFUL NATURE OF ABIGAIL

The fictional Abigail is very beautiful, aged seventeen, and shows 'an endless capacity for dissembling'. This capacity is clearly revealed during the progression of Act One and may be clarified by analysing her encounters with Reverend Parris, Reverend Hale and John Proctor.

Although Parris urges her to admit all the facts about the girls' activities in the forest, Abigail only pretends to state all she knows. Parris pleads with her, stating with dignity the seriousness of the situation and stressing the need for truth:

> PARRIS: Now tell me true, Abigail. And I pray you feel the weight of truth upon you, for now my ministry's at stake, my ministry and perhaps your cousin's life. Whatever abomination you have done, give me all of it now, for I dare not be taken unaware when I go before them down there.

> ABIGAIL: There is nothin' more. I swear it, uncle.

However, when questioned later by Reverend Hale, it becomes evident she knows that 'something more' than 'common dancing' has taken place at the nocturnal meetings in the forest. Her revelations, leading to the incrimination of Tituba, show a dissembling so extensive on Abigail's part that considerable lying is necessary to support the appearance she wishes to present. She has lied to her benefactor Parris, despite his emphasis on the need for truth, and soon this capacity is to be used for incriminating other innocent people.

Superficially, she is anxious to pretend about her 'name', or reputation for integrity. Rumours of a relationship with John Proctor have circulated since her dismissal from service in the Proctor household. Parris has requested her to tell him the truth about this possible blemish on her reputation:

> PARRIS: Your name in the town—it is entirely white, is it not?

> ABIGAIL (*with an edge of resentment*): Why, I am sure it is, sir. There be no blush about my name.

She attributes any aspersion cast on her character to Elizabeth Proctor. Abigail claims that John's wife has tried to treat her like a slave and she pretends that she has rebelled against such an attitude, asserting, in a temper:

> My name is good in the village! I will not have it said my name is soiled! Goody Proctor is a gossiping liar!

But in the brief, dramatically tense dialogue between Abigail and John when they are alone with the sick child, their past adulterous relationship is made explicit. In this encounter Abigail is shown not only to have lied to her guardian but also to possess a passionate, desiring nature. She has a shrewd percipience in seeing John's weakness and an active willingness to manipulate this man to satisfy her own passion. She reminds him of his own deeply emotional nature, recalling their sexual experience; she asserts that he is no 'wintry' man, and attributes (accurately as will be seen later) qualities of coldness, weakness and lack of passion to Elizabeth. . . .

THE PASSION OF ABIGAIL

Abigail displays a remarkable firmness of purpose. Her passion, now frustrated by John's return to sexual fidelity, is a driving force—a violent, pent-up power which has given her temporary influence over Proctor and a larger influence over the other girls. She is the leader among them. When urged by Mary Warren to tell the truth about their activities in the forest and provoked further by Betty's garblings, she reasserts her domination by an act of violence. She takes the sick child who has wandered from the bed to the window and 'smashes her across the face'. It is this tendency to violence which most deeply characterizes Abigail. The imagery she uses to describe imaginatively her sexual experience with Proctor suggests the mating of wild, hot, untamed animals:

> I know how you clutched my back behind your house and sweated like a stallion whenever I come near! Or did I dream that? . . . A wild thing may say wild things. But not so wild, I think. . . I have a sense for heat, John, and yours has drawn me to my window. . . I cannot sleep for dreamin'; I cannot dream but I wake and walk about the house as though I'd find you comin' through some door. (*She clutches him desperately.*)

Fulfilled passion may have offered a healthful integration of her emotions but, since John's rebuttal of her advances, the psychological violence is to break out into new manifestations. The extension of dissembling and lying is to arouse her innate violence and require increasing use of this disintegrative force. Unfortunately, the disintegrative force enters the community; other people's reputations are to be blemished, while Abigail's reputation for 'goodness' ironically grows.

Can any defence be made of such a person? It is important to remember that as a child she witnessed the murder of her parents:

> I saw Indians smash my dear parents' heads on the pillow next to mine, and I have seen some reddish work done at night.

The impression of violence and its ineradicable finality

seem to have remained with her. As an adolescent, to prose-cute her private vengeance against Elizabeth Proctor, she connives at judicial murder. And this may seem no unnat-ural thing to Abigail. The success of her first denunciations, the later trickery to implicate Elizabeth by means of the doll, and her supreme commanding power in the courtroom merely convince her that the form of verbal violence she has by chance discovered is an extremely effective weapon. So effective is it, and so great is her final power in suggesting the violent presence of diabolical disorders, that she can perturb even Deputy Governor Danforth.

THE POWER OF ABIGAIL

During the trial in Act Three, when Mary Warren has denied seeing spirits and, by implication, is invalidating the testi-mony of the girls, Danforth urges her to re-consider her pre-vious statements. However, his suggestion that she may, un-intentionally, have harboured illusions is rejected by Abigail as a 'base question'. Her following utterances are vehement expostulations which contain further images of violence:

> ABIGAIL: I have been hurt, Mr. Danforth; I have seen my blood runnin' out! I have been near to murdered every day because I done my duty pointing out the Devil's people—and this is my reward? To be mistrusted, denied, questioned like a—

> DANFORTH (*weakening*): Child, I do not mistrust you—

The all-powerful Danforth, for a moment, is made defensive; at this, Abigail asserts herself yet more by adopting an ac-cusatory attitude to the Deputy Governor:

> ABIGAIL (*in an open threat*): Let *you* beware, Mr. Danforth. Think you to be so mighty that the power of Hell may not turn *your* wits? Beware of it!

Shortly afterwards, when Proctor openly accuses *her* of plotting Elizabeth's death and enacting the vengeance of a whore, Danforth asks her if she will deny these charges. Abi-gail replies: 'If I must answer that, I will leave and I will not come back again!' The judge falters before this new disclo-sure and seems ready to doubt Abigail's evidence; at this point she steps up to him and asks, 'What look do you give me?' Danforth is unable to speak.

She is at the height of her power and can easily terrorize over Mary Warren's 'peeping courage'. When she manipulates the girls in the court, she is able to make Danforth 'horrified' so that even he grows hysterical. In these encounters with her, his responses have been characterized by self-defensiveness, reduction to silence, and finally a degree of hysteria.

ABIGAIL'S DESTRUCTIVE POWER

In this excerpt from The Crucible, *Abigail uses her power and influence to intimidate her friends.*

ABIGAIL: Now look you. All of you. We danced. And Tituba conjured Ruth Putnam's dead sisters. And that is all. And mark this. Let either of you breathe a word, or the edge of a word, about the other things, and I will come to you in the black of some terrible night and I will bring a pointy reckoning that will shudder you. And you know I can do it; I saw Indians smash my dear parents' heads on the pillow next to mine, and I have seen some reddish work done at night, and I can make you wish you had never seen the sun go down! *She goes to Betty and roughly sits her up.* Now, you—sit up and stop this!

But Betty collapses in her hands and lies inert on the bed.

MARY WARREN, *with hysterical fright:* What's got her?

Abigail stares in fright at Betty. Abby, she's going to die! It's a sin to conjure, and we—

ABIGAIL, *starting for Mary:* I say shut it, Mary Warren!

Abigail is a figure of human malevolence who, in the ironic reversals of humanistic values dramatized through the play's movements, is thought by some villagers and by the theocratic moral self-righteousness of the authorities to be a victim of circumstances. In one sense she may be such a victim: a luckless introduction to violence by the deaths of her parents has strengthened her will; her 'endless capacity for dissembling' has developed her art of duplicity so that, at the height of mass hysteria, she is a creature of supreme arrogance. John Proctor's words about Abigail—'She is a lump of vanity, sir'—suggest a fundamental truth about her nature. Were it not for her power of life and death over many people, she is a person to be pitied rather than condemned.

The atmosphere in the Proctor household is strained, and its tensions and uncertainties are implied by several dramatic devices at the beginning of Act Two. Before any words are uttered, John's actions, prior to Elizabeth's entry, are indicative of a deficiency in their relationship. He walks to the fireplace, tastes some stew and finds it unsatisfactory. Not wishing his wife to know this, he adds some salt and moves away from the fireplace before she comes into the room. He then compliments his wife on her cooking: 'It's well seasoned.' Elizabeth blushes with pleasure: 'I took great care.' The deceit is small, but even such a trivial hypocrisy may not be necessary in a well-balanced marital relationship; the consciousness of trying to please implies an unbalance which each is attempting to correct. Their actions and conversation show, in Miller's words, 'a sense of their separation', which has widened because of John's adultery with Abigail—an offence of extreme gravity in a puritan community.

This casts, as it were, a shadow over their relationship. Miller suggests this condition, when the couple speak together for the first time, by using the device of a seasonal metaphor. Although it is springtime, they live in a dark domesticity, symbolized by 'the low, dark, and rather long living-room' of the stage-setting. John has been out planting near the forest; now the farm is seeded. The implication made by associating farm with children is of a 'seeding' also in their marital relationship: 'Aye, the farm is seeded. The boys asleep?' As an audience learns later, Elizabeth is pregnant, and husband and wife now hope for a 'fair summer' which will make their farm and lives grow to fulfilment. John asserts in a moment of temporary optimism:

> It's winter in here yet. On Sunday let you come with me, and we'll walk the farm together; I never see such a load of flowers on the earth.

But the 'wintry' shadow quickly falls again when there is mention of Abigail and the extension of her prestige in the village:

> She speak of Abigail, and I thought she were a saint, to hear her. Abigail brings the other girls into the court, and where she walks the crowd will part like the sea for Israel.

Ironically, John and Elizabeth (and an audience) know Abigail's appearance of saintliness and innocence contrasts with her sexual knowledge and desire to connive at Elizabeth's downfall.

THE SUSPICION OF ELIZABETH

In the unbalanced domestic situation the mere name of Abigail helps to separate husband and wife once more. John mentions that he was alone with her for a short time in Reverend Parris's house, and Elizabeth's suspicions are irrationally aroused. The atmosphere in the room changes from illusory optimism to suspicion and anger.

ELIZABETH: You were alone with her?

PROCTOR (*stubbornly*): For a moment alone, aye.

ELIZABETH: Why, then, it is not as you told me.

PROCTOR (*his anger rising*): For a moment, I say. The others come in soon after.

ELIZABETH (*quietly—she has suddenly lost all faith in him*): Do as you wish, then. (*She starts to turn.*)

PROCTOR: Woman. (*She turns to him.*) I'll not have your suspicion any more. . .

ELIZABETH: Then let you not earn it.

John's anger rises and, in an emotional torrent, charges that she forgets nothing, forgives nothing and has little charity; he accuses her of being like a judge presiding in the court of their home. Elizabeth in reply insists, as she is to insist in the last meeting with her husband before his execution:

> I do not judge you. The magistrate sits in your heart that judges you. I never thought you but a good man, John—only somewhat bewildered.

She possesses a sharp psychological insight into his character. Aware that Abigail 'thinks to kill me, then to take my place', she warns her husband: 'You have a faulty understanding of young girls'—an observation which has been demonstrated by his encounter with Abigail in Act One and is to be further demonstrated by his treatment of Mary Warren.

In contrast to Abigail, who is characterized in part by her willingness to lie, the thought of deliberate lying is repugnant to Elizabeth, and one of the remarkably effective climaxes in Act Three is built upon this principle in her nature. During the trial, John states to Deputy Governor Danforth, 'That woman will never lie.' He repeats the assertion later:

> In her life, sir, she have never lied. There are them that cannot sing, and them that cannot weep—my wife cannot lie.

Then, in an effort to protect John's reputation, Elizabeth sacrifices the principle she holds most dear: she lies and, by the terrible irony of the situation, assists in the condemnation of her husband.

The period of physical separation and imprisonment, during which her pregnancy takes its course, effects a change in her. When she visits John before his execution, she refuses still to judge him, although she is confronted with a situation to which her fundamental principle is opposed. John, to save his life, considers the possibility of lying by signing a confession of his guilt. She is quietly resolute in the face of this possibility:

> It is not my soul, John, it is yours. Only be sure of this, for I know it now: Whatever you will do, it is a good man does it.

Perhaps her resolution has come from thinking upon John's 'goodness'; this, the confounding of her own principle in the courtroom, and the condition of pregnancy have induced her to read her heart. As a consequence, she has become aware of a past 'coldness' in her attitude to her husband.

ELIZABETH'S MOVEMENT TO SELF-KNOWLEDGE

As a girl she had thought herself so plain that she feared she might never marry; so deep had been this sense of inadequacy that, when John did offer her marriage, she was suspicious of him. It was this suspiciousness—a central trait in her character—underlying her 'coldness' which may have impelled her husband to seek the warm arms of Abigail. He is no 'wintry' man, and therefore could not be profoundly happy within a 'wintry' relationship. In cadenced prose, possessing the tautness of poetry, Elizabeth finally reveals to John with pathetic frankness this aspect of herself:

> I counted myself so plain, so poorly made, no honest love could come to me! Suspicion kissed you when I did; I never knew how I should say my love. It were a cold house I kept! ... Forgive me, forgive me, John—I never knew such goodness in the world!

Elizabeth has found a new deeper knowledge through tribulation and a process of self-examining. Unjust accusation, her husband's imperilling himself to save her, her own unintended condemnation of John, imprisonment and pregnancy—have all contributed to this painful self-knowledge; but most important, perhaps, in the social dimensions of the drama, is the awareness, to one who abominates lying, that consistent, reiterated and public mendacity can compound disorder and make what is unnatural or evil seem morally right and just. Against this reversal of values, a person can only seek and live by an inner 'goodness'. With this discovery, Elizabeth's basic insecurity—her wondering, feminine suspiciousness—is reduced: a profounder awareness replaces negative suspicion. Like her husband in the final moments of his life, she has her goodness now and no human force can take it away.

A Comparison of *The Crucible* and *Death of a Salesman*

Robert Hogan

In his comparison of *The Crucible* and *Death of a Salesman*, Robert Hogan suggests that *Death of a Salesman* is a better play because it evokes greater emotions. He argues, however, that *The Crucible* has greater dramatic power in its plot and that its theme emerges more clearly from the action. Of the two heroes, Hogan writes that John Proctor in *The Crucible* attains a peace found in self-knowledge whereas Willy Loman in *Death of a Salesman* dies passive and uncomprehending. Proctor reflects human triumph whereas Willy demonstrates failure.

Robert Hogan teaches English at the University of California, Davis. He is an editor and author of several books on modern drama, including *The Experiments of Sean O'Casey*.

Miller is a slow, painstaking, and deliberate writer who sometimes composes thousands of pages to get a hundred that are right. Consequently, . . . *The Crucible* did not appear until January 22, 1953. It was generally thought a sound work but a lesser one than *Death of a Salesman*. In its original run it achieved only 197 performances, but its off-Broadway revival several years later played well over 500. Its merits were at first overshadowed by the notoriety of its most obvious theme. The subject of the play, the Salem witch trials of 1692, was distractingly applicable to what has been called the witch hunts of the 1950's. Now, when the most impassioned fervor of Communist hunting has abated, the play may probably be judged on its own merits, unobscured by newspaper headlines.

The Crucible is a strong play, and its conclusion has much

From *Arthur Miller* by Robert Hogan. University of Minnesota Pamphlets on American Writers, no. 40 (Minneapolis: University of Minnesota Press, 1964). Copyright ©1964 by the University of Minnesota. Reprinted by permission of the publisher.

of the force of tragedy. It has not the permeating compassion of *Death of a Salesman,* but there is more dramatic power to John Proctor's death than there was to Willy's. It is a harder hitting play, and its impact stems from Proctor's death being really a triumph. You cannot pity a man who triumphs. Willy Loman's death was a failure, and his suicide only a gesture of defeat. Him you can pity.

THE CRUCIBLE AS A MORE DRAMATIC PLAY THAN DEATH OF A SALESMAN

The Crucible is really a more dramatic play than *Death of a Salesman.* The earlier play attempted to construct a plot about Willy's losing his job, and Biff's attempting to gain one, but these strands of plot were only a frame on which to hang the exposition of a man's whole life. The plots of *Death of a Salesman* are not the center of the play, but in *The Crucible* the action is the play's very basis, its consuming center. One watches *Death of a Salesman* to discover what a man is like, but one watches *The Crucible* to discover what a man does. *Death of a Salesman* is a tour de force that succeeds despite its slim action because its real center is the accumulation of enough significant detail to suggest a man. In the life of John Proctor, one single action is decisive, dominating, and totally pertinent, and this action, this moment of decision and commitment, is that climax toward which every incident in the play tends. *Death of a Salesman* is not traditionally dramatic, at least in the Aristotelian sense that the center of a drama is an action. *The Crucible* is so dramatic, and the centrality of its plot explains its greater strength.

That strength is also explained by the clarity with which the theme of *The Crucible* emerges from its plot. The theme of *Death of a Salesman* does not emerge so much from its story as from its illustration and exposition. For that reason it is necessary for Linda and Charley in their laments to explain the meaning of Willy's life, and actually Linda is still explaining what the play means in the last scene. *The Crucible* requires no such exposition, for the play's meaning has been acutely dramatized. The exposition in *Death of a Salesman* is dramatic only in the way that the keening in *Riders to the Sea* is dramatic. It is a lyrical evocation of emotion rather than a dramatic one.

The Crucible is more traditionally dramatic in one other way. The theme of a play is made more intense by the hero's either making a discovery of past folly (Oedipus, Lear) or being presented with an agonizing dilemma (Orestes, Hamlet). Proctor's story has elements of both situations. His past folly, which he has been trying unsuccessfully to live down, is his seduction of Abigail Williams, and this fault eventually destroys him when Abigail turns against him and accuses him of witchcraft. The center of the play, however, is his dilemma about commitment. This dilemma is stated in each act in somewhat different terms. In Act I, Proctor washes his hands of the town's problem and refuses to be involved in the absurd charges of witchcraft being made by a small group of frightened, hysterical girls. In Act II, he is pushed into involvement when Abigail denounces his wife Elizabeth as a witch. In Act III, he attempts legally to rescue the accused, but by resorting to law also attempts to avoid being involved himself. Finally, at the end of the act, he can only achieve justice by involvement, and so he accuses Abigail and becomes himself one of the accused. Proctor's identification with the accused is not yet total. He drags his feet as did Lawrence Newman. He suffers with them for months in prison, but in the final moment before his execution he signs a confession of witchcraft. His reason is that he is really different from them. He cries: "I cannot mount the gibbet like a saint. It is a fraud. I am not that man. My honesty is broke, Elizabeth; I am no good man. Nothing's spoiled by giving them this lie that were not rotten long before." Proctor is still striving for a compromise, but Miller will allow him none. Proctor signs the confession to save his life, but the judges demand that the confession be made public, and he finds that he cannot live in society uncommitted. He must be either totally and publicly against the accused or totally and publicly with them. There is no middle ground of private commitment and public neutrality. This is Proctor's final dilemma as it was Lawrence Newman's[1] and Joe Keller's,[2] and Miller will not, at this point in his career, allow the individual to escape from his social obligation into his private life.

Willy Loman Compared with John Proctor

Two points connect this situation with the tradition of austere tragedy. First, an individual is pushed to definition, forced to irreclaimable and self-destructive action. That self-

1. protagonist in *Focus*   2. protagonist in *All My Sons*

destruction is, paradoxically, an affirmation of morality, for it asserts that belief is more important than life. Second, the individual discovers his need to choose, and his agony comes from his awareness. Reason, said Milton, is but choosing, and Proctor's aware choice is the choice of a reasoning man. That last point indicates the distance between Proctor's tragedy and Willy Loman's. Willy's is a kind of passive, uncomprehending, mute, brute suffering. Whatever peace Willy attains by his death is the peace of oblivion, but whatever peace Proctor attains is the peace of knowledge. Willy's is a pathetic tragedy, Proctor's an austere one. Willy's story arouses pity, Proctor's suffering. Willy's death is a lament for the destruction of value, Proctor's a paean to its creation. And finally, Willy's is the story of man's failure, and Proctor's the story of man's triumph.

Technically the play is not as interesting as *Death of a Salesman* or as tightly structured as *All My Sons*. Its structure is, however, appropriate for the retelling of the witch hunt story and for the revelation to Proctor of the need for commitment. Its language is not as lyrically evocative as that of *Death of a Salesman*, but it does not need to be. In *Death of a Salesman* language had to be a substitute for plot; here it can be unobtrusively subservient. Actually the dialogue of the play is a considerable accomplishment. It suggests the flavor of seventeenth-century speech without becoming distractingly archaic and without sacrificing simplicity, strength, or suppleness.

Death of a Salesman may always be considered a better play than *The Crucible* for two reasons. First, there were no distracting headlines to hurt the initial impact of the earlier play, and the American theater is so commercially and journalistically oriented that even a later success can rarely erase the first impression. Second, and even more important, the emotions evoked by the pathetic tragedy are closer to the surface than those aroused by the austere one. Hamlet is a fuller and more intelligent view of humanity than is Cyrano and Proctor than Willy, but they will never arouse as many tears. The fault is not in the playwright but in the naiveté of his form, and the naiveté of his form is dictated by the naiveté of his audience—in other words, by human nature.

CHAPTER 5

Other Works

READINGS ON
ARTHUR MILLER

An Introduction to *All My Sons*

Hersh Zeifman

Hersh Zeifman suggests that *All My Sons*, like much of Arthur Miller's work, is influenced by the realism of Norwegian playwright Henrik Ibsen. In the tradition of Ibsen, the play's central theme is the need to find a sense of belonging to both the family and society. Zeifman argues that despite the play's intricate plot and powerful emotional impact, it has some of the predictable elements of soap opera that disqualify it as a great drama. As Miller's first successful play, *All My Sons* is important because it contains the major themes that Miller would explore throughout his career.

Hersh Zeifman is an associate professor of English at York University, Toronto. He is the coeditor of *Modern Drama* and president of the Samuel Beckett Society. He is the author of numerous articles on modern drama.

All My Sons, Arthur Miller's first Broadway success, centres on the Keller family: father Joe, mother Kate, son Chris. A manufacturer of military airplane parts during World War II, Joe Keller was convicted (but later exonerated on appeal) of knowingly shipping out defective cylinder heads, resulting in the deaths of 21 American P-40 pilots. The catalyst for the play's action is Chris's startling announcement that he intends to marry Ann Deever, the daughter of Joe's former business partner (on whom Joe had placed the blame for his war-time crime and who is currently serving a jail sentence) and the fiancée of Chris's younger brother, Larry, an airforce pilot who has been missing in action for three years. Kate, unable to accept Larry's death, is adamant that Chris and Ann never marry. As the play progresses, a series of long-buried secrets is gradually brought to light: Chris discovers that Joe is guilty of the crime of which he stood accused; all three Kellers discover that Larry is dead, having committed suicide out of shame over his father's treachery; and, most crucially, Joe discovers that there is something more important than the financial well-being of his immediate family (his reason for committing the crime)—a discovery that ultimately leads to his own suicide.

THE INFLUENCE OF HENRIK IBSEN

Structurally and thematically, *All My Sons* is heavily indebted to the plays of Henrik Ibsen, a major influence on all Miller's work. The intense Ibsenite realism of *All My Sons*, where the ghosts of the past return both to haunt the present and to shape its future, is immediately evidenced in the minutely detailed setting of the Kellers' back garden—a setting which remains constant throughout all three acts. Miller obeys every possible unity in this early play. Thus the events of the play unfold during the course of a single August Sunday: one long day's journey into night. And to complete this neoclassical rigour, there is also unity of action: as in Ibsen, the play dramatizes a central ideological struggle, a literally life-and-death struggle of ethics and values. As Miller has commented: "Joe Keller's trouble . . . is not that he cannot tell right from wrong but that his cast of mind cannot admit that he, personally, has any viable connection with his world, his universe, or his society. . . . The fortress which *All My Sons* lays siege to is the fortress of unrelatedness".

The spokesman in the play for "relatedness", for a connection with the larger "family" of humanity, is Chris. As his name suggests, Chris is a metaphoric Christ, a secular "saint" espousing universal love for all God's children. "Chris, a man can't be a Jesus in this world", Joe cries out in anguished self-defence at the play's climax. But that is precisely what the idealist Chris demands. Joe's justification for his crime is the primacy of family: "I'm his father and he's my son", he says of Chris, "and if there's something bigger than that I'll put a bullet in my head!". For Chris, of course, there *is* something bigger than that; to believe otherwise is to abandon civilization to the beasts, to ethical chaos. However much he chooses to rationalize his crime, Joe is not divorced from his society, from the world at large: he has responsibilities to that world, to himself as a social (and

A Son Confronts His Father in *All My Sons*

As a result of businessman Joe Keller's decision to ship defective engine parts, twenty-one American pilots died in World War II. In this excerpt from All My Sons, *Joe is confronted by his son Chris. In it, the father reveals that he does not understand what Chris knows—that there is a responsibility greater and more important than making a living and providing for the material well-being of the family.*

CHRIS. I want to know what you did, now what did you do? You had a hundred and twenty cracked engine-heads, now what did you do?

KELLER. If you're going to hang me then I . . .

CHRIS. I'm listening, God Almighty, I'm listening!

KELLER. (*Their movements now are those of subtle pursuit and escape.* KELLER *keeps a step out of* CHRIS' *range as he talks*). You're a boy, what could I do! I'm in business, a man is in business; a hundred and twenty cracked, you're out of business; you got a process, the process don't work you're out of business; you don't know how to operate, your stuff is no good; they close you up, they tear up your contracts, what the hell's it to them? You lay forty years into a business and they knock you out in five minutes, what could I do, let them take forty years, let them take my life away? (*His voice cracking.*) I never thought they'd install them. I swear to God. I thought they'd stop 'em before anybody took off.

CHRIS. Then why'd you ship them out?

KELLER. By the time they could spot them I thought I'd have the process going again, and I could show them they needed me and they'd let it go by. But weeks passed and I got no kick-back, so I was going to tell them.

CHRIS. Then why didn't you tell them?

KELLER. It was too late. The paper, it was all over the front page, twenty-one went down, it was too late. They came with handcuffs into the shop, what could I do? (*He sits on bench at center.*) Chris . . . Chris, I did it for you, it was a chance and I took it for you. I'm sixty-one years old, when would I have another chance to make something for you? Sixty-one years old you don't get another chance, do ya?

therefore a *human*) being. "What the hell are you?", Chris demands of his father at the height of their confrontation: the key question in all of Miller's plays. Joe's ultimate answer is to walk off stage and put a bullet in his head, thereby both acknowledging his guilt and conceding the validity of

Chris's (and Larry's) moral vision: Larry killed himself because the pilots Joe sent to their deaths were, in a larger context, *all* his "sons".

A FLAWED BUT IMPORTANT PLAY

The debt to Ibsenite realism undoubtedly accounts for much
of the power of *All My Sons*: once caught up in its intricate
and relentless plot, an audience finds itself inevitably swept
along by the play's urgency and moral passion. At the same
time, however, Miller's relative immaturity as a playwright
occasionally betrays itself. For many critics, the play's sometimes creaky contrivances—a climactic letter from beyond
the grave; the denouement propelled by a slip of the tongue;
the sudden blurting out of long-buried truths for maximum
dramatic effect—smack of the worst excesses of the well-
made play, of soap opera. Further, while the play painstak-
ingly spells out Joe Keller's guilt, what about *Chris's* "guilt"?
Miller has shamelessly stacked the deck, allowing Chris to
hold all the moral cards and to exult in playing them. This
makes Chris, despite his status as Miller's alter ego and the
play's ethical *raisonneur* in many ways a difficult character
to admire: his idealism can so easily come across as smug
self-righteousness, as adolescent whining.

Still, for all its shortcomings, *All My Sons* is an important
play. In its focus both on the family and on the debunking of
the materialism and "success-at-any-price" aspects of a spiritually debased American Dream, it is typical not only of
much American drama in general but of the entire body of
Arthur Miller's theatrical work in particular. However much
they may vary stylistically, all Miller's plays explore the
same thematic ground: the conflict between, on the one
hand, individual identity and integrity (who are you? what
do you believe? what *should* you believe?), and, on the other,
the beliefs and values of American society at large—a conflict Miller first dramatized successfully, and rivetingly, here
in *All My Sons*.

Miller's Nontheatrical Work

Neil Carson

Arthur Miller's body of literary work includes, as well as plays, writings spanning genres from military reportage to short stories to screenplays. Despite the fact that these nontheatrical pieces offer important insights into the nature of Miller's art, they are often overlooked by the critics. Neil Carson analyzes three of Miller's nontheatrical writings: *Situation Normal*, a nonfiction profile of military life; *Focus*, a novel; and "The Misfits," a short story.

Neil Carson is associate professor of English at the University of Guelph in Ontario, Canada.

In the plays following *Death of a Salesman* Miller has tried in a variety of ways to overcome what he felt was a certain lack of comprehension on the part of his audience. His failure to find a form that would illuminate the issues that he saw underlying the events he dramatised led him to a period of self-doubt. He began to feel that in the works he had written for Broadway he had been little more than a 'kind of entertainer succeeding in drawing a tear or a laugh ... [but that] what was behind his plays remained a secret.' During the eight years or so that separated the London production of *A View from the Bridge* and the New York première of *After the Fall*, Miller continued to look for a way to unite in his drama the 'pervasive conditions of existence' with the 'hidden' laws that gave significance to that existence. But his efforts were disappointing and he found himself turning increasingly to non-dramatic forms, especially the short story. Miller had written reportage and fiction in the early 1940s, but during the period 1956–60 he was to find in the short story what almost amounts to a new voice. Quieter in tone, more intimate, less desperate in their striving after meaning, Miller's stories constitute a neglected aspect of his work. In his fiction we can see the author dealing with the ideas that concern him in his plays, but his treatment of these ideas is more subtle.

AN ANALYSIS OF *SITUATION NORMAL*

Such subtlety did not come immediately. In his first prose works we can see all too plainly the assumptions that underlie his early plays. *Situation Normal* (1944) is an account of Miller's investigation of American training bases undertaken as background for the screenplay of *The Story of G.I. Joe*. It is a series of vivid sketches of officers and enlisted men interspersed with reflections by the author which reveal little about the American fighting man, but a great deal about the young Arthur Miller. It is clear that Miller was anything but objective as a reporter. Because he himself saw the war so clearly as a crusade against fascism in defence of democracy and the principle of equality, he wanted the American soldiers to see it in the same light. But he had to admit that they did not. 'It is terrible to me that everything is so personal. . . . I can't seem to find men who betray a social responsibility as a reason for doing or not doing anything.' Because of his own convictions, however, Miller could not accept the evidence of his senses. So he attributed to the men a kind of subconscious understanding of the war which they could not express. 'I am beginning to think that perhaps those beliefs are there in a totally unsuspected guise.' Some justification for this hope was supplied by a veteran soldier by the name of Watson who was failing his officer's training course because of a sense of disorientation after combat. Explaining the pressures of battle, Watson said,

> You find out all about yourself out there, as if all the excuses you've always made for yourself were suddenly very silly. Friendship is the greatest thing out there. . . . I tell you the truth: I would die for any one of thirty or forty men out there just as easy as I'd flick out this match.

Miller magnified this sense of loyalty and unit pride into something more mystical. 'No man', he claims, 'has ever felt identity with a group more deeply and intimately than a soldier in battle.' In that state, Miller suggests, there is complete equality, a common aim, no little prejudices or selfish aims, and everyone gains a sense of 'exhilaration' from the knowledge that he is helping an enormous mass of men toward a great and worthy goal. The kind of purposeful and unified society produced by danger, he feels, can also be created by a 'commonality of Belief'. The sceptical might reflect that this vision of common purpose perhaps owes as much to socialist idealism as it does to direct observation, but there is no doubt that it was an important part of Miller's belief at the time.

MILLER REFLECTS ON HIS FAMILY

In his autobiography, Timebends, *Arthur Miller, a Jew, writes that in the 1920s his family tried to blend into mainstream America, downplaying their religious heritage. Ultimately, they were shaken out of their denial by the depression and World War II.*

In the twenties, when [my father] flourished, the Ku Klux Klan was riding high, swelling its membership immensely from year to year, and the Jews were their prime targets where there were few Negroes to threaten. The time was still far off when racism and bigotry would seem anything but natural and even praiseworthy ideas equated with patriotism and pride of ancestry. If ever any Jews should have melted into the proverbial pot, it was our family in the twenties; indeed I would soon be dreaming of entering West Point, and in my most private reveries I was no sallow Talmud reader but Frank Merriwell or Tom Swift, heroic models of athletic verve and military courage. As it turned out, we were building a fortress of denial that would take two massive onslaughts to crack—the Depression and Hitler's war.

The second conviction was his sense that without a clear idea of why he had fought and what he had accomplished, the returning American veteran would become a prey to the destructive tendencies in American life. Opposed to the ideal of community in the foxholes, Miller saw the evil of a society of selfish competition in which each person tries to exclude his neighbours. In such a society, unless the returning soldier's attachment to his home was overwhelming, 'he was going to feel the loss of a social unit . . . a social goal worth his sacrifice'. The only thing which could rejoin the soldier with America was a 'Belief in the rightness, the justness, the necessity of his fight' which he could share with all civilians. Without such a belief, Miller feared, the returning soldier would be lost, restless, and an easy prey to demagogues. . . .

AN ANALYSIS OF *FOCUS*

In his second major prose work, the novel *Focus* (1945), Miller addresses the questions of belief and communication in a different context. The activities of the Christian Front, a violently anti-Semitic group which became active in New York towards the end of the war, seemed to confirm Miller's fears that individuals without an understanding of why the war had been fought were susceptible to antisocial demagogy. Miller was interested in tracing the process by which an individual might move from blindness to understanding. *Focus* deals with the awakening of social conscience in a gentile when he suddenly experiences for himself the effects of anti-Semitism. Lawrence Newman is a personnel officer in a large New York office who is responsible for enforcing the company policy against hiring Jews. When he buys himself a badly needed pair of glasses he begins to be taken for a Jew himself, and when the supervisor tries to move him to a less conspicuous office he resigns in indignation. He is finally taken on by a Jewish firm where he encounters a woman he had previously refused to hire on the mistaken assumption that she was Jewish. Seeing her now in an entirely different light he falls in love with her and marries her. Following his purchase of glasses, and increasingly after his marriage, Newman is subjected to pressures to join a movement to force a Jewish merchant away from the Brooklyn neighbourhood in which Newman lives. Prompted by his wife who realises that they must either join with the Christian Front or be attacked by it, Newman attends a Front rally. There he is mistaken for a Jew and thrown out. A couple of nights later, in the company of his wife, he is attacked by a group of young toughs. The attack coincides with an attack on the Jewish merchant, and Newman and Finklestein find themselves fighting side by side until they finally drive off their assailants. Newman reports the attack to the police who also mistake him for a Jew. Realising at last the true brotherhood of man, he allows the mistake to go uncorrected.

The novel is rather too contrived to be entirely believable psychologically. The metamorphosis of Newman is a clever technical device to emphasise the superficiality of the causes of prejudice, and the unreliability of sight as a means of knowing someone. The early cautious and apprehensive Newman is especially well drawn, but it seems improbable that such a man could become transformed into the resolute fighter of the second half of the novel. Characteristically Miller introduces sex as an important subsidiary theme, but the story of Newman's courtship and marriage is not fully explored, nor is its relevance to the main theme at all clear. Nevertheless, *Focus* is an extremely interesting work for what it reveals about certain fundamental political and psychological assumptions of the author.

Underlying the title and the central image of the spectacles is the belief that people do not really see one another. Newman comes to understand Finklestein as a man (rather than as a stereotype) as a result of two incidents. First he shares Finklestein's experience when he himself suffers from anti-Semitism. But more important, he is made to understand the Jew when Finklestein turns on him in anger.

> Standing there looking into his angry face, Newman's idea of him altered. Where once he had seen a rather comical, ugly, and obsequious face, now he found a man, a man throbbing with anger. And somehow his anger made him comprehensible to Mr. Newman.

I'm not sure that this is believable psychology, but it is closely related to Miller's fervent conviction that no man should allow himself to be victimised. There is a recurring refusal on the part of Miller's characters to accept without question the outside world's assessment of their character or motives. This refusal arises from the need these characters feel to justify or explain themselves (or, as Miller expresses it, to 'evaluate themselves justly'). Although Miller sees this characteristic as a universal human need, felt most strongly by the tragic hero, it seems more likely to be the experience of a member of a minority group facing the prejudice or indifference of the majority. . . .

AN ANALYSIS OF 'THE MISFITS'

A peculiarity of these early works is the essentially masculine nature of the communal ideal. In both prose works the male world of action, sacrifice and loyalty is contrasted with the female world of subjectivity, timidity and selfishness. Although Gertrude in *Focus* embodies a number of female characteristics (few of them attractive), it is her final desertion of Newman when the latter is being attacked that is most significant. In Miller's terms, her lack of physical courage is a symbol, not a cause, of her 'sin of incomprehension.' In his later work Miller comes to realise that his earlier views had been rather too simplistic. But until very late, his vision of the world reflects some curious anti-feminine biases.

An interesting transitional work in which the ideal of male comradeship is held up for scrutiny is 'The Misfits', a short story written in 1957 about his experiences in Nevada when he spent six weeks there prior to filing for divorce [from his first wife, Mary Grace Slattery]. In the story, Gay Langland, Perce Howland and Guido Racanelli are three itinerant cowboys who make a living at a variety of odd jobs. As the tale opens they are working respectively as a gigolo, a rodeo rider and a garage mechanic. But these occupations are temporary. The work that gives Gay and Guido the most satisfaction, and the labour by which they choose to define themselves, is the hunting of wild mustangs. Once an honourable occupation needed to supply riding ponies and breeding stock for the farms and ranches in the region, the hunt has degenerated into a sordid pursuit of the small remnants of the once vast herds for sale to the processors of dogfood. The three men view the hunt differently. Guido, a callous veteran of many bombing missions during the Second World War, takes pride in the technical aspects of the hunt—the pursuit by plane and truck, and the use of heavy tyres to capture the horses—all of which are his inventions. Gay rather stolidly persists in the enterprise maintaining that what he is doing has not changed, but that society has demeaned his labour. Perce, the youngest, is the only one to respond to the suffering of the horses themselves, or to perceive any tragedy in their destruction. But they all agree that the hunt is 'better than wages', and somehow convince themselves that it represents an honourable alternative to enslavement by a commercial society. In the end, Perce's scruples are quelled as he agrees to accompany the others to Thighbone Mountain to ferret out the last survivors of the wild herds.

Miller's portrayal of this pathetic group of 'misfits' is brilliantly ambiguous. On the one hand, they represent the last of a dying breed of men whose courage and spirit of independence recall the days of the American frontier. Huge as it was, that frontier had a sense of community and common purpose which had even then been destroyed in other parts of America. In the west the community transcended family. It was an 'endless range . . . and it connected [a man] sufficiently with his father and his wife and his children. . . . [Gay felt that] he had neither left anyone nor not-left as long as they were all alive on those ranges.' In such a world, family life is pleasant (Gay remembers his home as the best part of his life), but it is essentially limiting—'a stake to which [one is] pleasurably tethered'. On the other hand, Miller shows with a restrained irony the limitations of these 'heroes'. None of the men is capable of seeing his actions as having any larger significance. Since the death of his wife and baby, Guido has lost his ability to love, and the sense of 'loose gaiety' he feels is a symptom of his lack of sense of purpose. Gay is immature, with boyish facial features and an adolescent's need to do things which he cannot explain or justify logically. Perce is also young with a young man's sensitivity, but totally lacking in ambition and will-power. These men have refused to accept the conventional role of wage-earner that American society attempts to impose on its members. But . . . unlike Newman and Finklestein, they have not found their dignity. Instead they have themselves become victimisers, enslaving and destroying the mustangs to avoid enslavement by the capitalist system.

Miller's balance of sympathy in 'The Misfits' is evidence of a much more complex understanding of the problem of individual integrity. It is true that the men's work has been turned to corrupt ends by a commercial society, but is there not something in the men that has collaborated in that corruption? Are the cowboys trapped or free? The story ends with a long and detailed description of the captured horses. The adults stand roped to the heavy tyres, helplessly awaiting their fate.

> From time to time the stallion caught the smell of the pastures [in the mountains] and he started to walk toward the vaulted fields in which he had grazed; but the tire bent his neck around, and after a few steps he would turn to face it and leap into the air with his forelegs striking at the sky, and then he would come down and be still again.

The 'misfit' horses are obviously a symbol of the misfit men, and the image of their helplessness is both pitiable and outrageous. But there is one horse, the colt, which is unfettered and confined only by something in its nature. On the way back to town Gay asks Perce if he is going to join him on the hunt in Thighbone Mountain. 'Okay,' Perce says and goes back to sleep. In a symbolically parallel situation, the colt, although free to leave the captured mare, does not.

When the first pink glow of another morning lit the sky the colt stood up, and as it had always done at dawn it walked waywardly for water. The mare shifted and her bone hoofs ticked the clay. The colt turned its head and returned to her and stood at her side with vacant eye, its nostrils sniffing the warming air.

'The Misfits' constitutes a sombre picture of man's relationship to society in that it recognises the relentless power of inner forces working against freedom and self-realisation. In this story, belief and knowledge are not enough if they are unsupported by sensitivity and will.

CHRONOLOGY

1914–1918

World War I

1915

Arthur Miller is born in New York City, the second of three children of Isidore and Augusta Barnett Miller; Arthur has an older brother, Kermit, and a younger sister, Joan, will be born in 1921

1917–1920

Russian Revolution

1921

Miller's sister, Joan born

1928

Isidore Miller's business fails and the Miller family moves to Brooklyn

1929

The New York stock market crash and the start of the Great Depression

1933

Arthur graduates from high school to a number of odd jobs; while working as a shipping clerk, he discovers literature, including the influential Russian novel *The Brothers Karamazov* by Fyodor Dostoyevsky; President Franklin D. Roosevelt introduces New Deal reforms

1934

Miller enrolls at the University of Michigan

1936

Miller's first play, *No Villain*, wins University of Michigan's Avery Hopwood Award for drama

1937

Miller's play *They Too Arise*, a revised version of *No Villain*, earns a prize from the Theatre Guild Bureau of New Plays and his *Honors at Dawn* wins Avery Hopwood Award

1938

Miller graduates with a degree in English; moves back to New York and writes scripts for the Federal Theatre Project

1939–1945

World War II and the Holocaust

1940

Miller marries his college sweetheart, Mary Grace Slattery

1941

Japan bombs Pearl Harbor, December 7

1944

Miller's first child, Jane, is born; Miller tours army camps and writes a book of military reportage, *Situation Normal.* His first drama to play on Broadway, *The Man Who Had All the Luck*, closes after only six performances

1945

Miller's novel *Focus* is published; first atomic bomb is dropped on Hiroshima; Japanese surrender ends WWII in the Pacific

1947

Miller's second child, Robert, is born; after many drafts, Miller's play *All My Sons* is produced; 328 performances later, the play wins the New York Drama Critics Circle Award

1949

Death of a Salesman opens in New York City; wins the Pulitzer Prize and the Antoinette Perry Award; Miller also publishes "Tragedy and the Common Man," the first of many essays on the nature of drama

1950–1953

Korean War

1950

Miller meets actress Marilyn Monroe; he writes an adaptation of Henrik Ibsen's play *An Enemy of the People*; Mc-Carthyism and the Red Scare take hold in Washington

1953

The Crucible opens on Broadway

1955

Miller begins a relationship with Marilyn Monroe; writes *A View from the Bridge* and *A Memory of Two Mondays*

1956

Miller divorces Mary Slattery and marries Marilyn Monroe; he is subpoenaed to appear before the House Un-American Activities Committee (HUAC) and is cited for contempt of Congress; *A View from the Bridge* opens in London

1957

Miller's short story "The Misfits" appears in *Esquire* magazine; Miller also publishes *Collected Plays*; Soviet Union launches *Sputnik*, the first man-made satellite

1958

Miller's HUAC contempt conviction is reversed

1961

Miller's screenplay *The Misfits* is filmed starring Marilyn Monroe; Monroe and Miller divorce

1962

Miller marries photographer Inge Morath; Marilyn Monroe commits suicide; Cuban missile crisis

1963

President John Kennedy is assassinated in Dallas

1964

After the Fall opens in January and *Incident at Vichy* premieres in December; President Lyndon Johnson commits U.S. soldiers to the conflict in Vietnam

1965

Miller is elected president of the International Association of Poets, Playwrights, Editors, Essayists, and Novelists

1967

Miller publishes a collection of short stories, *I Don't Need You Anymore*

1968

The Price opens on Broadway; *Death of a Salesman* reaches sales of one million; Martin Luther King Jr. is assassinated in Memphis

1969

America lands a man on the moon

1970

Miller's works are banned in the Soviet Union as a result of his work to free dissident writers

1971

The Portable Arthur Miller is published

1972

The Creation of the World and Other Business opens and closes after twenty performances; Watergate scandal begins with burglary at Democratic Party national headquarters in Washington, D.C.

1974

Richard Nixon resigns U.S. presidency

1975

Miller works to free convicted murderer Peter Reilly; the last Americans are evacuated from Vietnam

1977

Miller petitions the Czech government to halt arrests of dissident writers; writes *The Archbishop's Ceiling*

1980

The American Clock premieres

1982

Miller writes two one-act plays, *Elegy for a Lady* and *Some Kind of Love*; Vietnam War memorial is unveiled in Washington, D.C.

1983

Miller and his wife travel to China to see a production of *Death of a Salesman* in Beijing

1984

Dustin Hoffman plays Willy Loman in a Broadway revival of *Death of a Salesman*; Ronald Reagan is elected to a second term as president

1985

Death of a Salesman airs on television to an audience of twenty-five million

1986

Miller writes *Danger: Memory!*

1987

Miller's autobiography, *Timebends: A Life*, is published

1990

Miller writes a screenplay for the motion picture *Everybody Wins*; President George Bush launches Operation Desert Storm against Iraq

1991

Miller's play *The Ride Down Mt. Morgan* opens in London; dissolution of the Soviet Union

1993

Miller's comedy-drama *The Last Yankee* premieres in New York

FOR FURTHER RESEARCH

BIOGRAPHICAL WORKS AND
INTERVIEWS WITH THE PLAYWRIGHT

Bernard Dekle, "Arthur Miller," *Profiles of Modern American Authors*. Rutland, VT: Tuttle, 1969, pp. 147–53.

Richard I. Evans, *Psychology and Arthur Miller*. New York: E.P. Dutton, 1969.

Bruce Glassman, *Arthur Miller*. Englewood Cliffs, NJ: Silver Burdett, 1990.

Jean Gould, "Arthur Miller," *Modern American Playwrights*. New York: Dodd, Mead, 1966, pp. 247-63.

John Gruen, "Arthur Miller," *Close-Up*. New York: Viking, 1968, pp. 58-63.

Elia Kazan, *Elia Kazan: A Life*. New York: Knopf, 1988.

Arthur Miller, *Timebends: A Life*. New York: Grove Press, 1987.

Benjamin Nelson, *Arthur Miller: Portrait of a Playwright*. New York: David McKay Company, 1970.

Matthew Roudane, ed., *Conversations with Arthur Miller*. Jackson: University Press of Mississippi, 1987.

ABOUT ARTHUR MILLER'S PLAYS

Harold Bloom, ed., *Modern Critical Views: Arthur Miller*. New York: Chelsea House, 1987.

John H. Ferres, ed., *Twentieth-Century Interpretations of* The Crucible. Englewood Cliffs, NJ: Prentice-Hall, 1992.

Ronald Hayman, *Arthur Miller*. New York: Ungar, 1972.

Robert A. Martin, ed., *Arthur Miller: New Perspectives*. Englewood Cliffs, NJ: Prentice-Hall, 1982.

Walter J. Merserve, ed., *The Merrill Studies in* Death of a Salesman. Columbus, OH: Merrill, 1972.

Leonard Moss, *Arthur Miller, Revised Edition.* Boston: Twayne Publishers, 1980.

Brenda Murphy, *Miller:* Death of a Salesman. Cambridge, England: Cambridge University Press, 1995.

C.J. Partridge, *The Crucible (Arthur Miller).* Oxford: Basil Blackwell, 1971.

Matthew Roudane, ed., *Approaches to Teaching Miller's* Death of a Salesman. New York: The Modern Language Association, 1995.

June Schlueter and James K. Flanagan, *Arthur Miller.* New York: Ungar Publishing, 1987.

Dennis Welland, *Arthur Miller: A Study of His Plays.* London: Methuen, 1979.

Sidney Howard White, *The Merrill Guide to Arthur Miller.* Columbus, OH: Merrill, 1970.

HISTORICAL BACKGROUND

Thomas Adler, *American Drama, 1940–1960: A Critical History.* New York: Twayne Publishers, 1994.

Gerald M. Berkowitz, *American Drama of the Twentieth Century.* London: Longman, 1992.

C.W.E. Bigsby, *Modern American Drama, 1945–1990.* Cambridge, England: Cambridge University Press, 1992.

Kenneth C. Davis, *Don't Know Much About History.* New York: Avon Books, 1990.

David Halberstam, *The Fifties.* New York: Fawcett Columbine, 1993.

Frederick Lumley, *Trends in 20th Century Drama.* New York: Oxford University Press, 1960.

George Jean Nathan, *Theatre in the Fifties.* New York: Knopf, 1953.

G.J. Watson, *Drama: An Introduction.* New York: St. Martin's Press, 1983.

WORKS BY ARTHUR MILLER

Arthur Miller's works are available in a wide variety of anthologies and reissues; therefore, facts of publication are omitted from the following list. All works are plays unless otherwise noted.

No Villain (1936)

Situation Normal (journal); *The Man Who Had All the Luck* (1944)

Focus (novel) (1945)

All My Sons (1947)

Death of a Salesman (1949)

Adaptation of Henrik Ibsen's *An Enemy of the People* (1950)

The Crucible (1953)

A View from the Bridge; *A Memory of Two Mondays* (1955)

Collected Plays (1957)

The Misfits (the screenplay) (1961)

After the Fall; *Incident at Vichy* (1964)

I Don't Need You Anymore (short stories) (1967)

The Price (1968)

The Creation of the World and Other Business (1972)

The Archbishop's Ceiling (1977)

The American Clock (1980)

Elegy for a Lady; *Some Kind of Love* (1982)

Danger: Memory! (1986)

Timebends: A Life (autobiography) (1987)

The Ride Down Mt. Morgan (1991)

The Last Yankee (1993)

INDEX

185